STOP THE POLLUTION & INSPIRE PEOPLE TO PICK-UP WHIPPED CREAM CANISTERS OF NITROUS OXIDE JUNKIES AND MAKE EASTER DECORATIONS

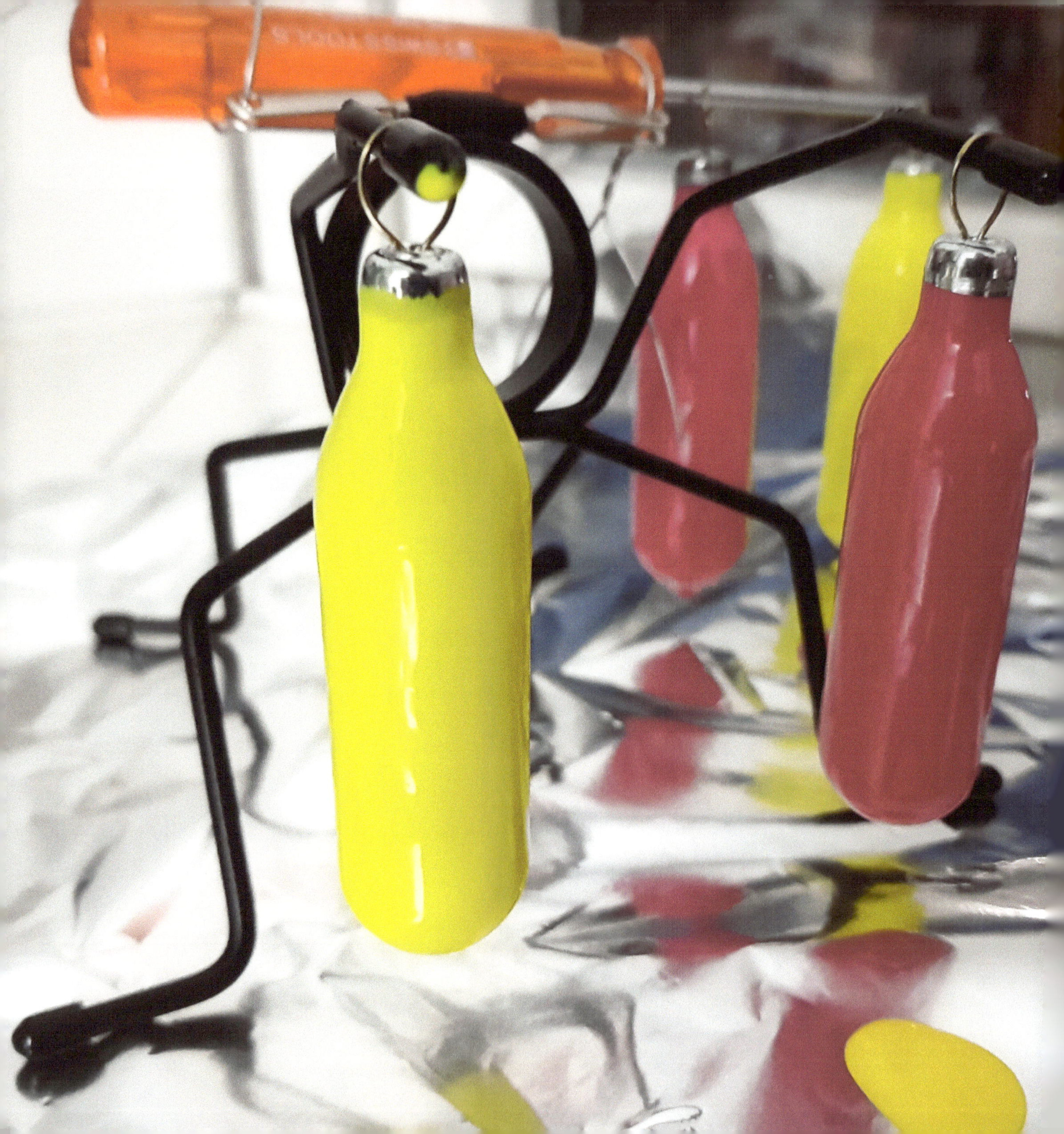

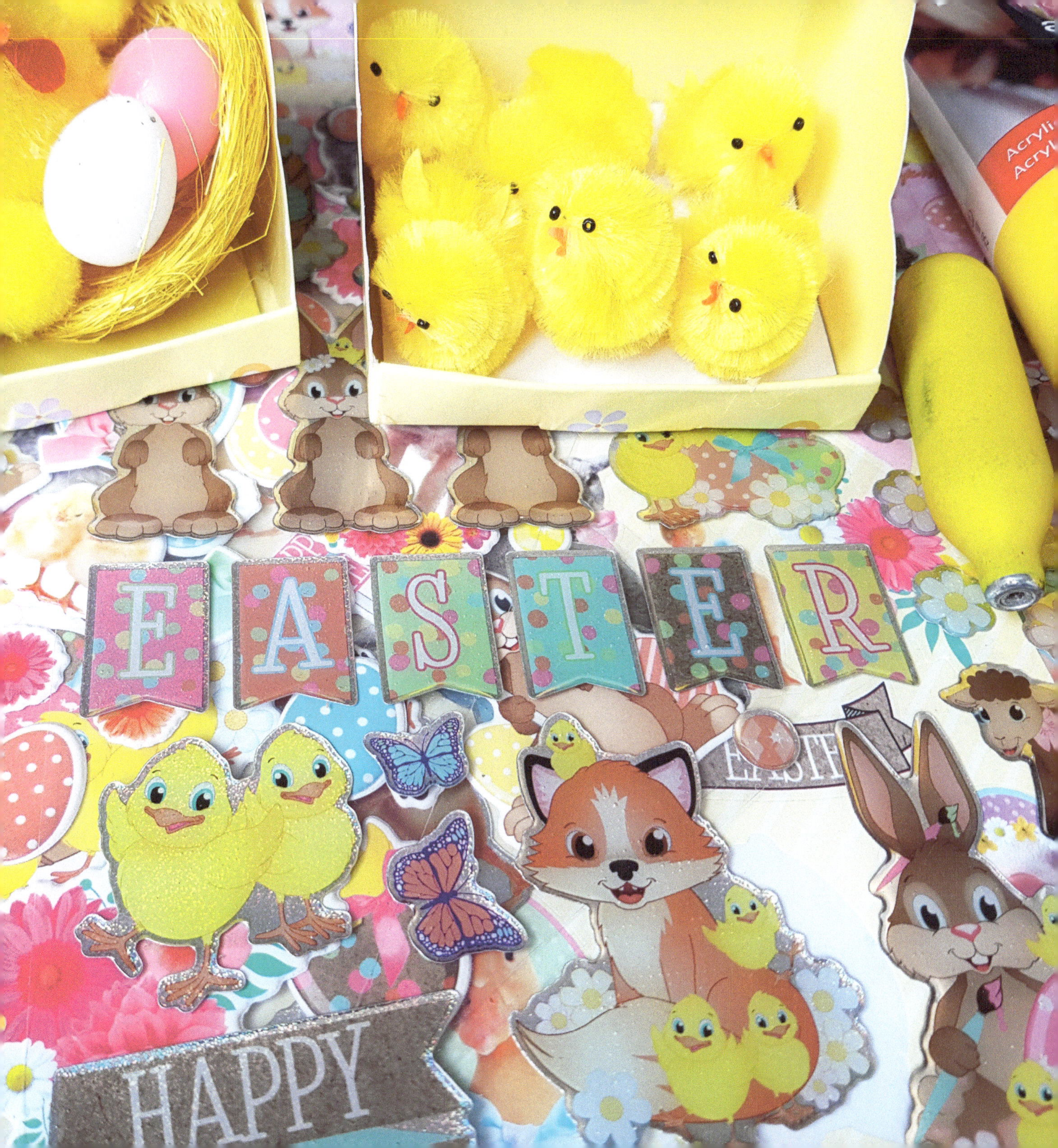
EASTER
HAPPY

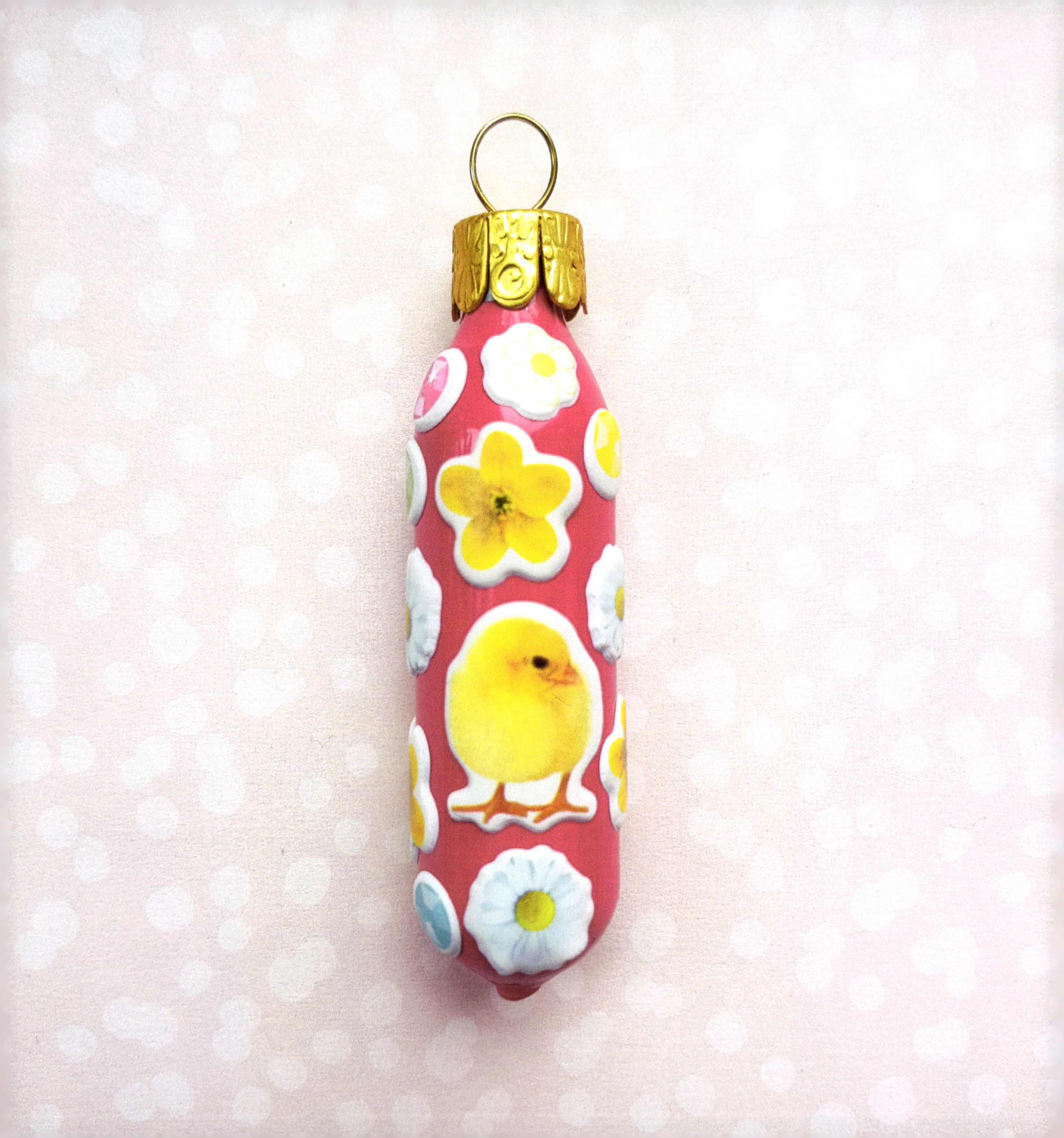

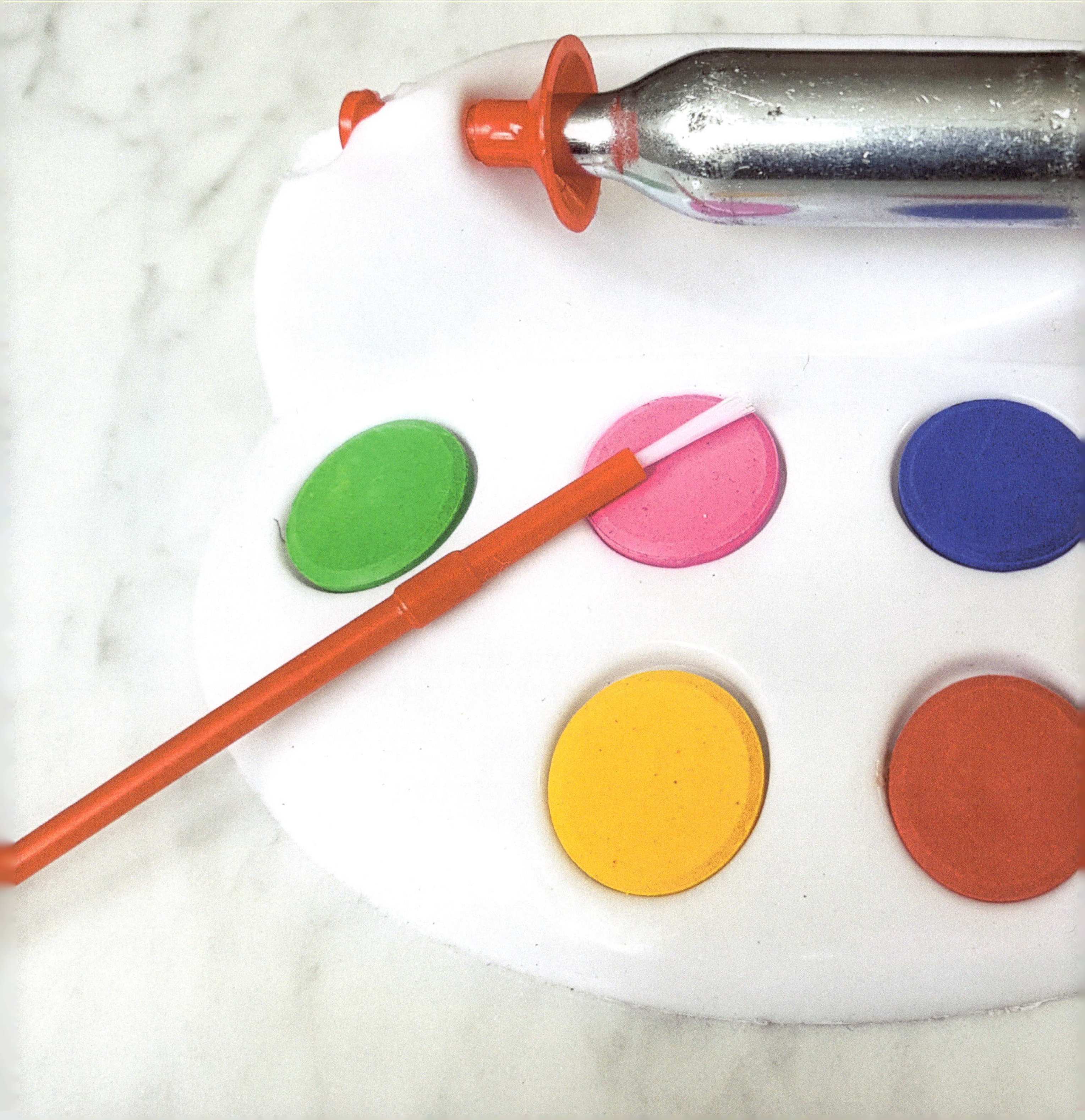

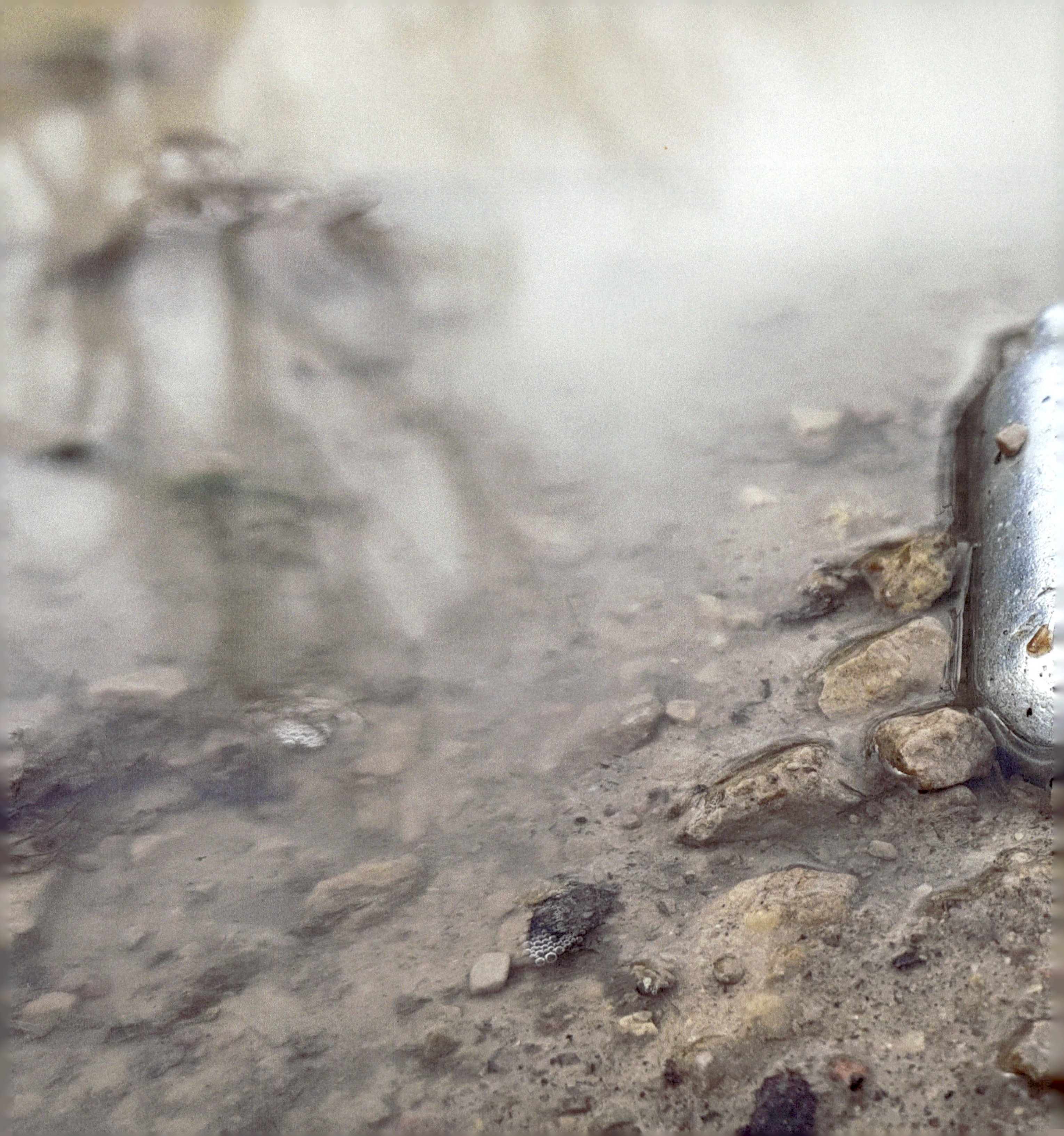

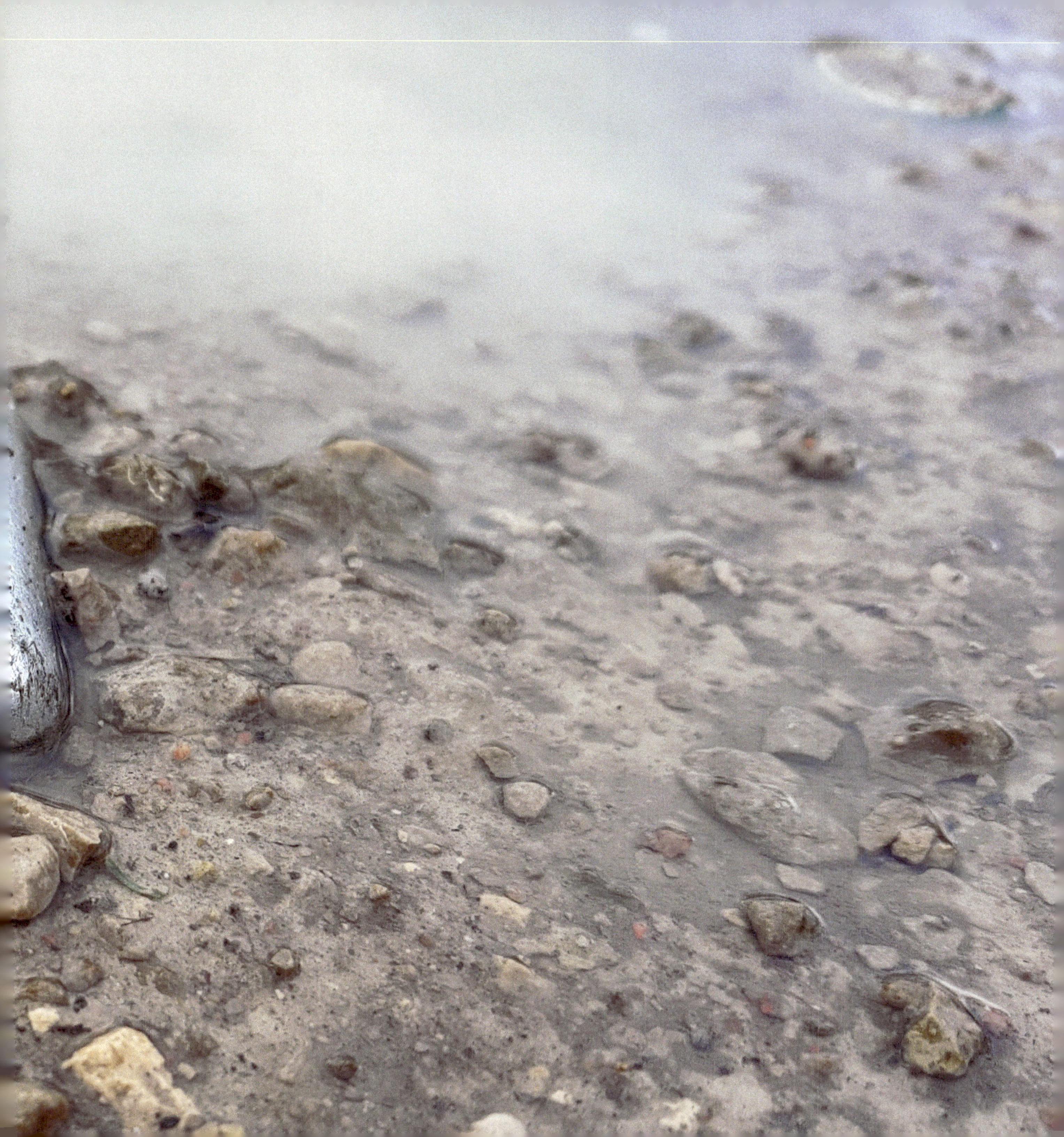

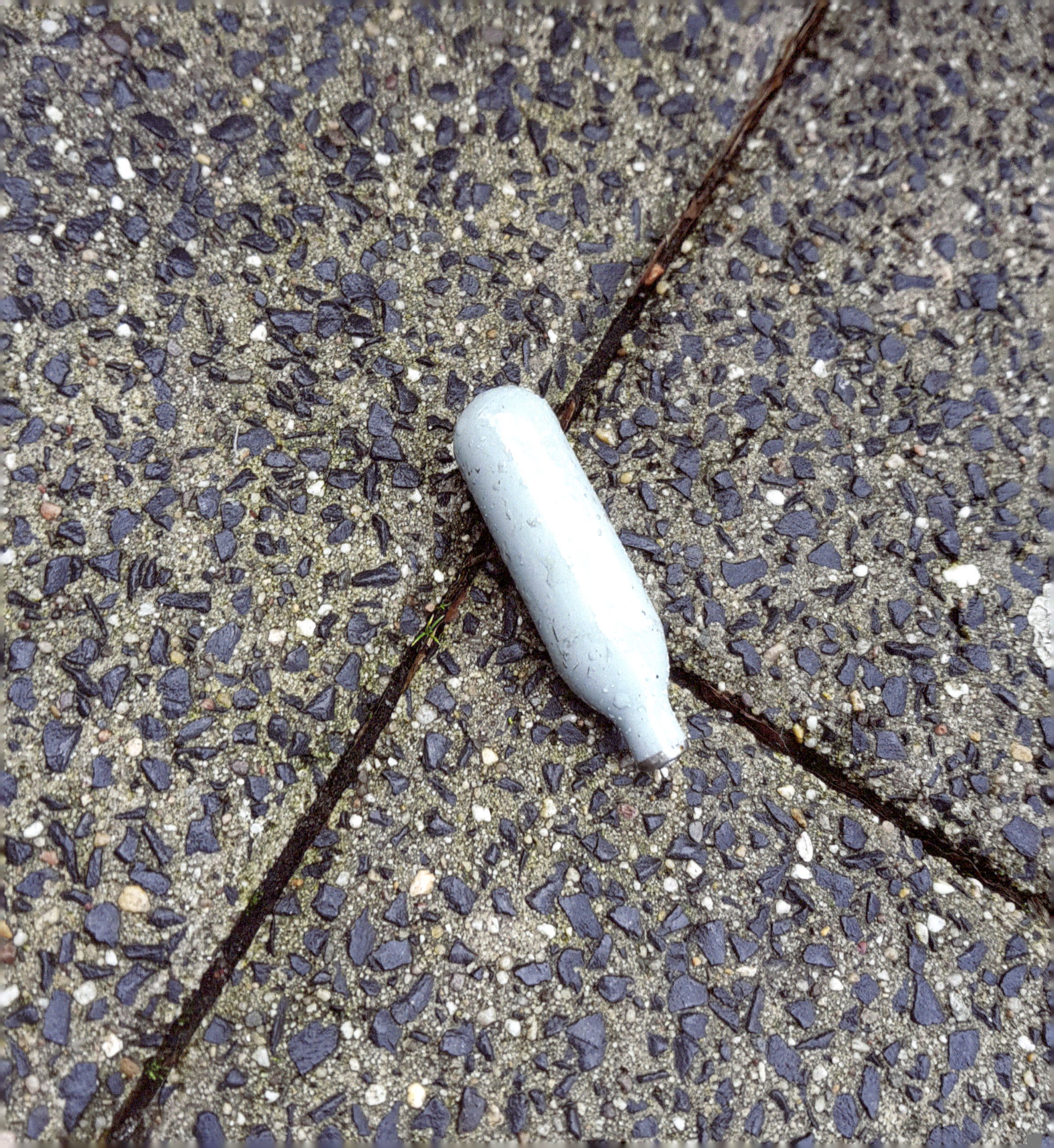

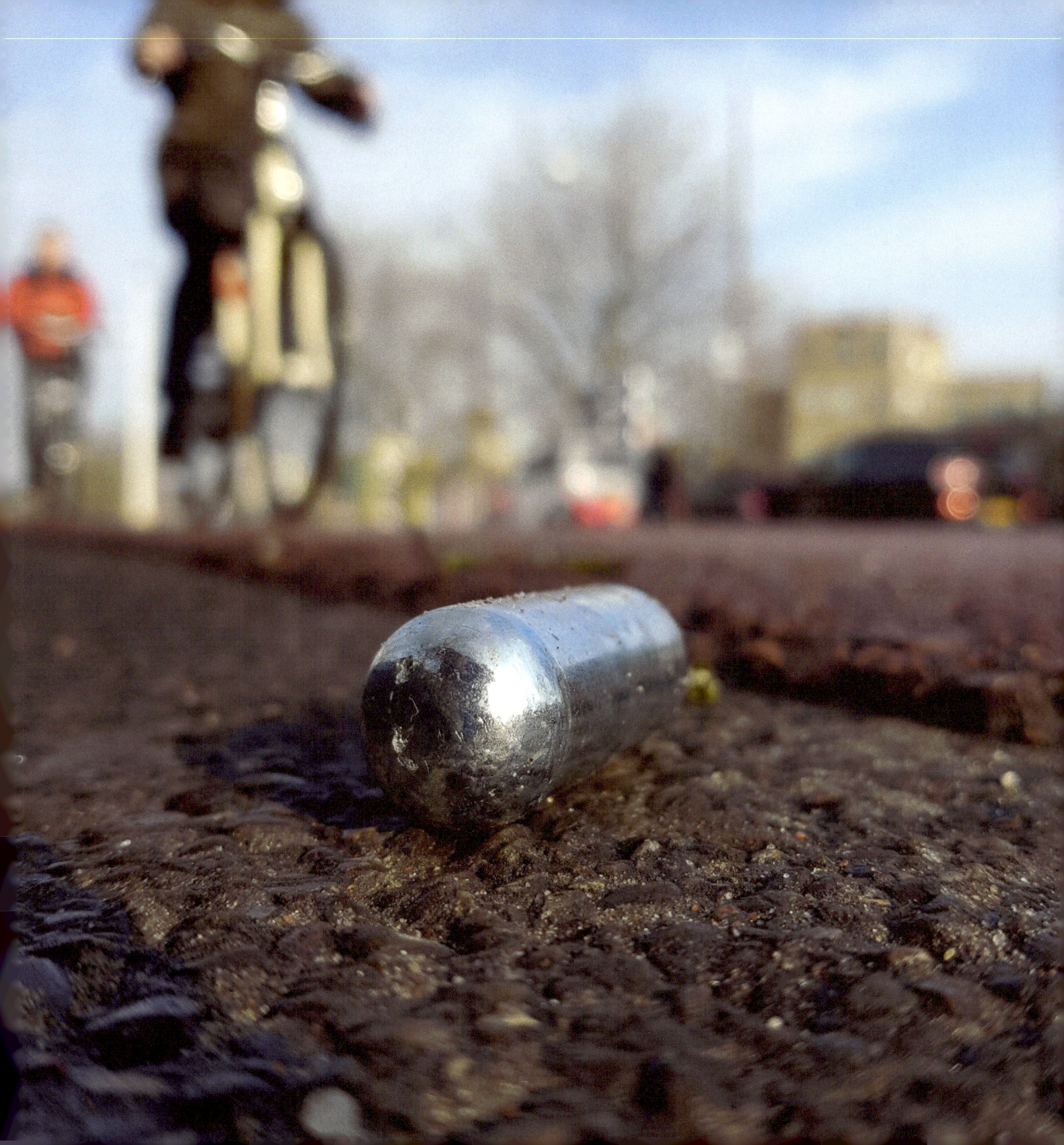

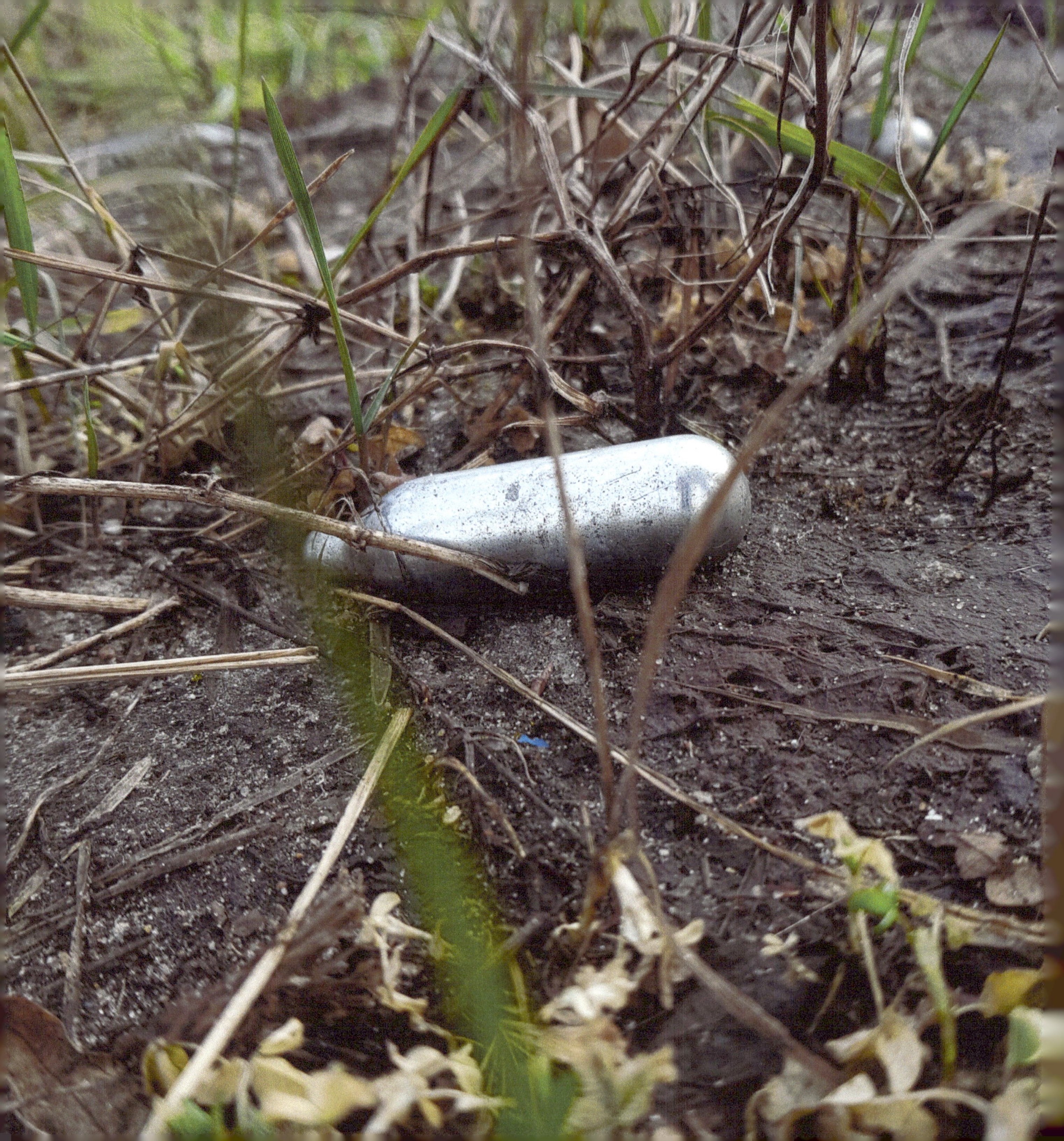

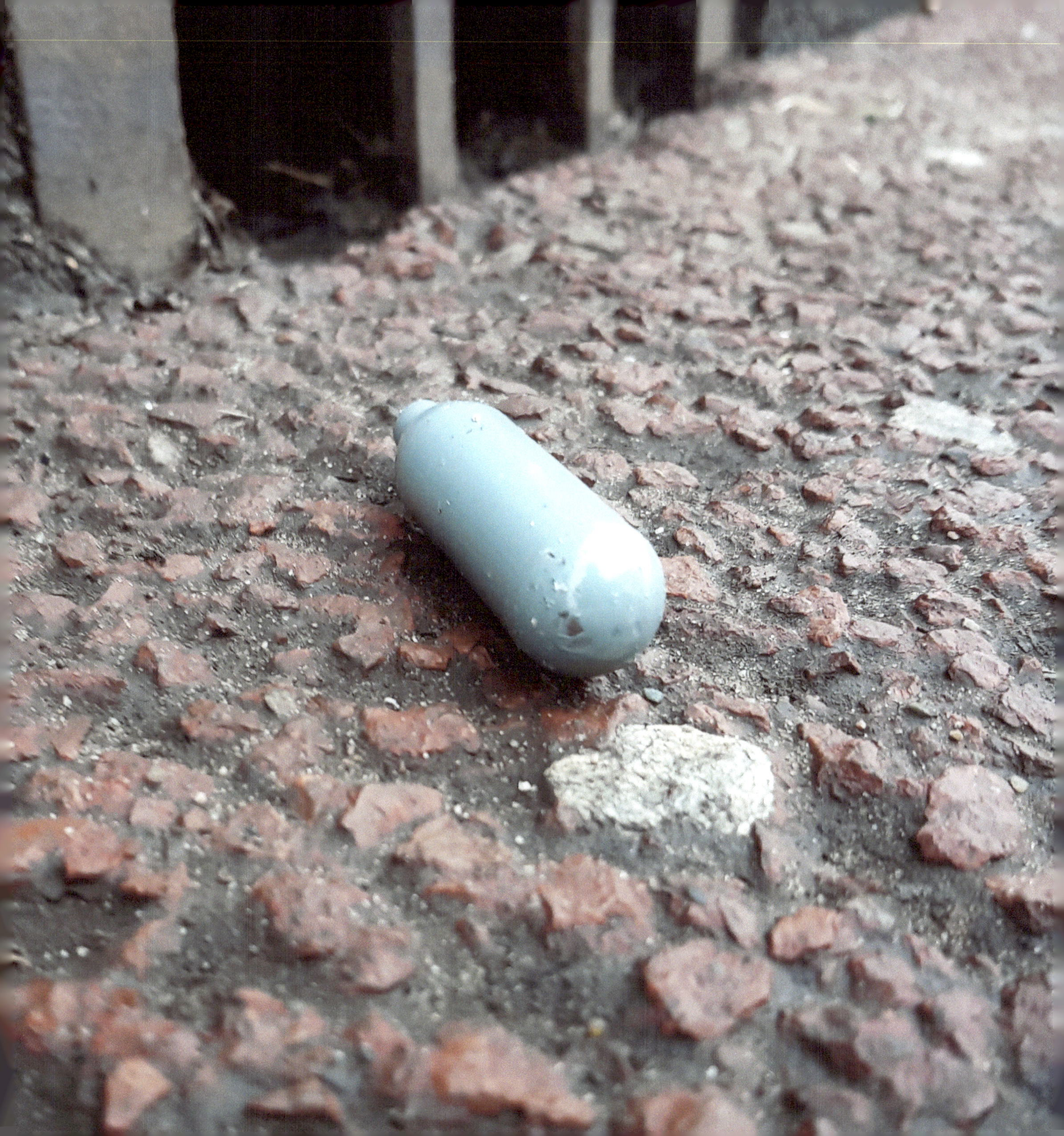

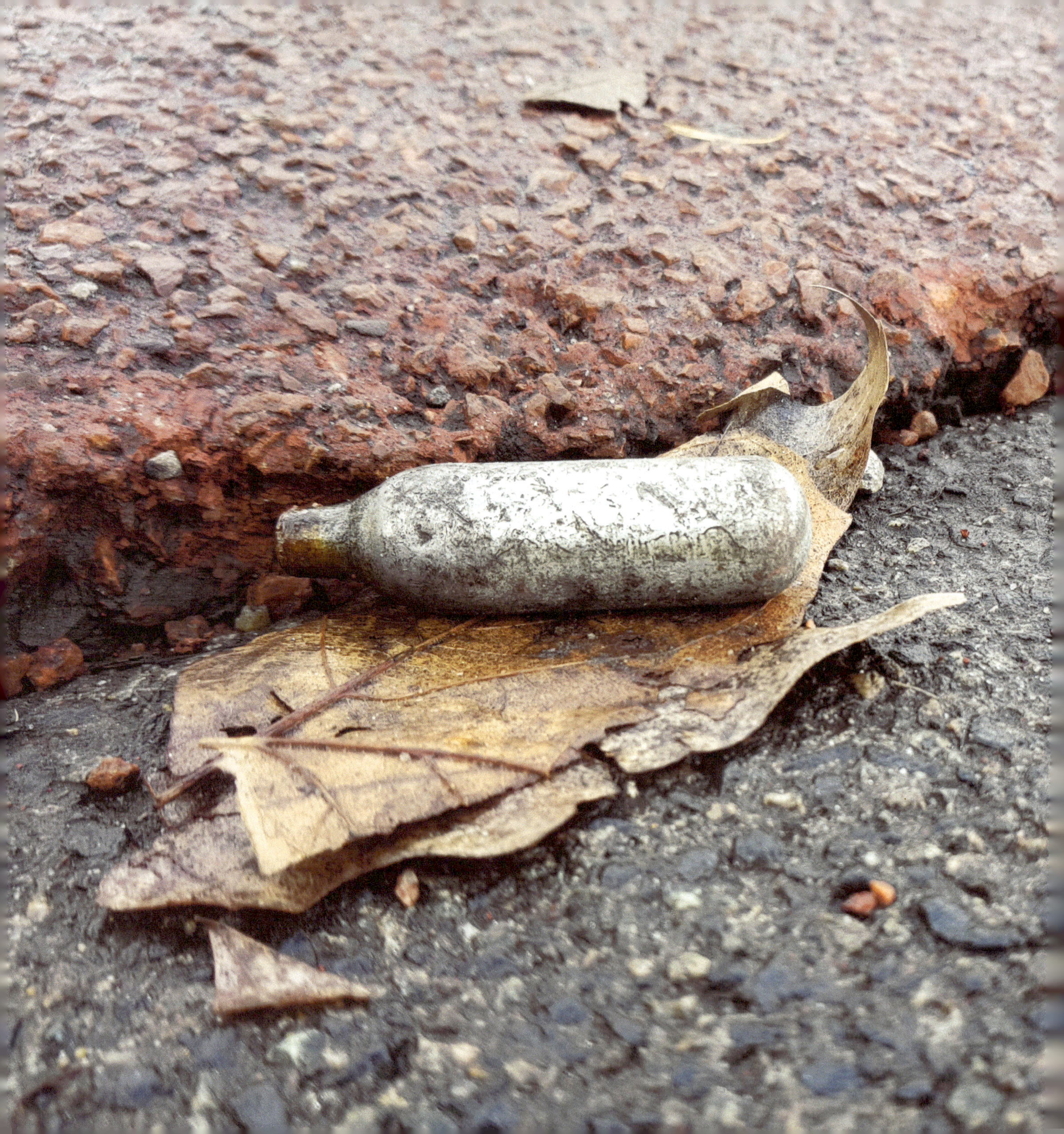

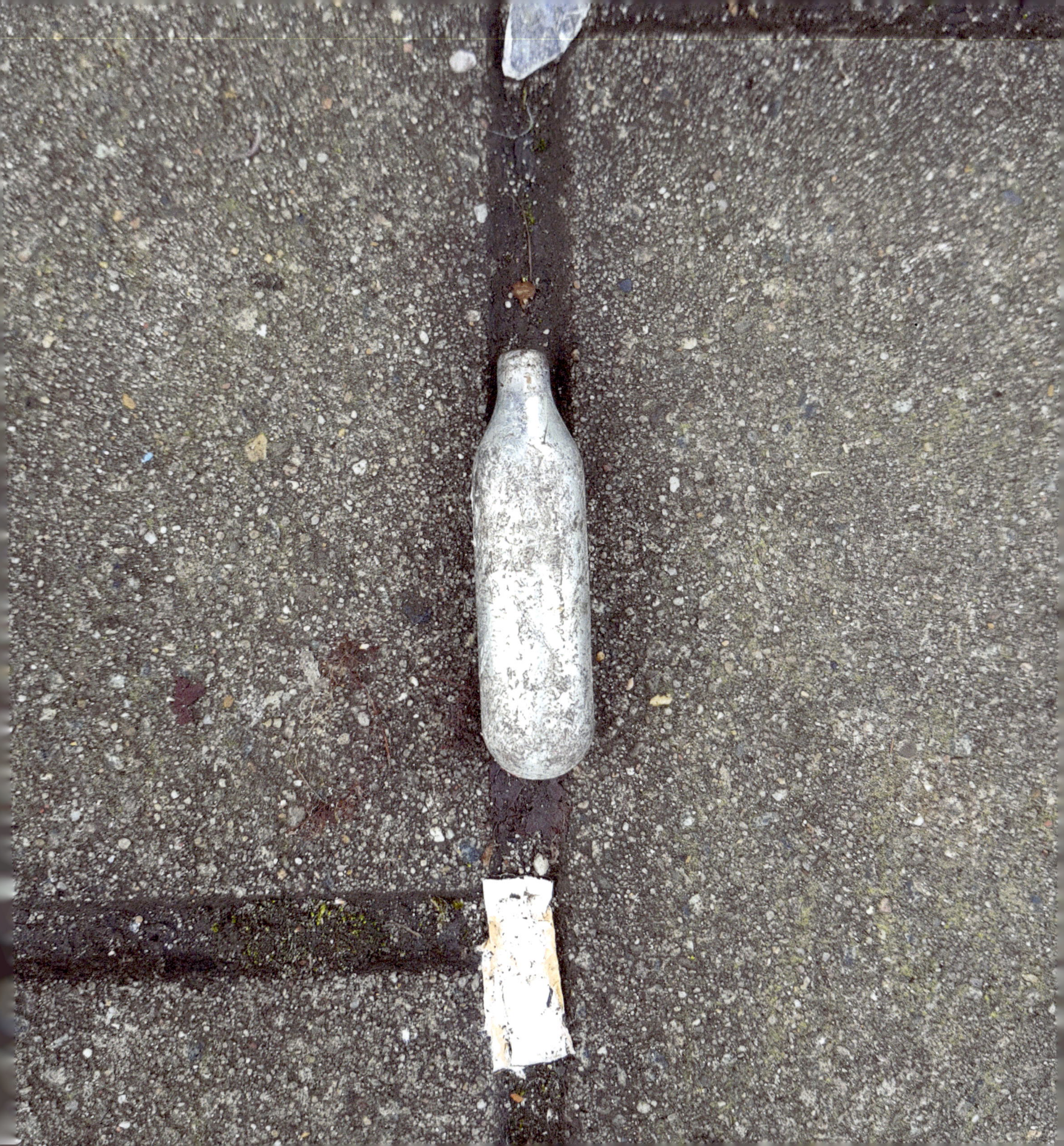

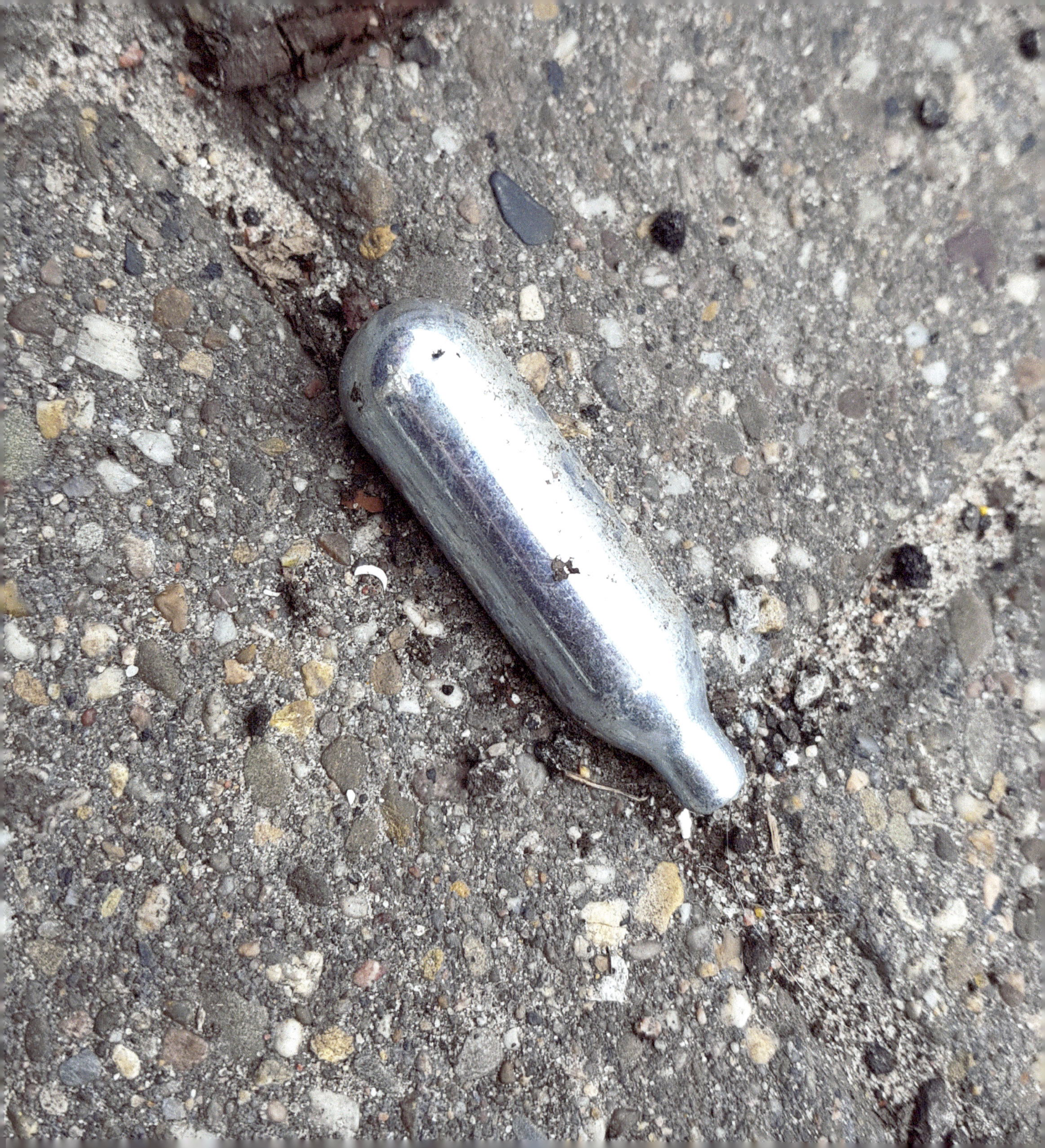

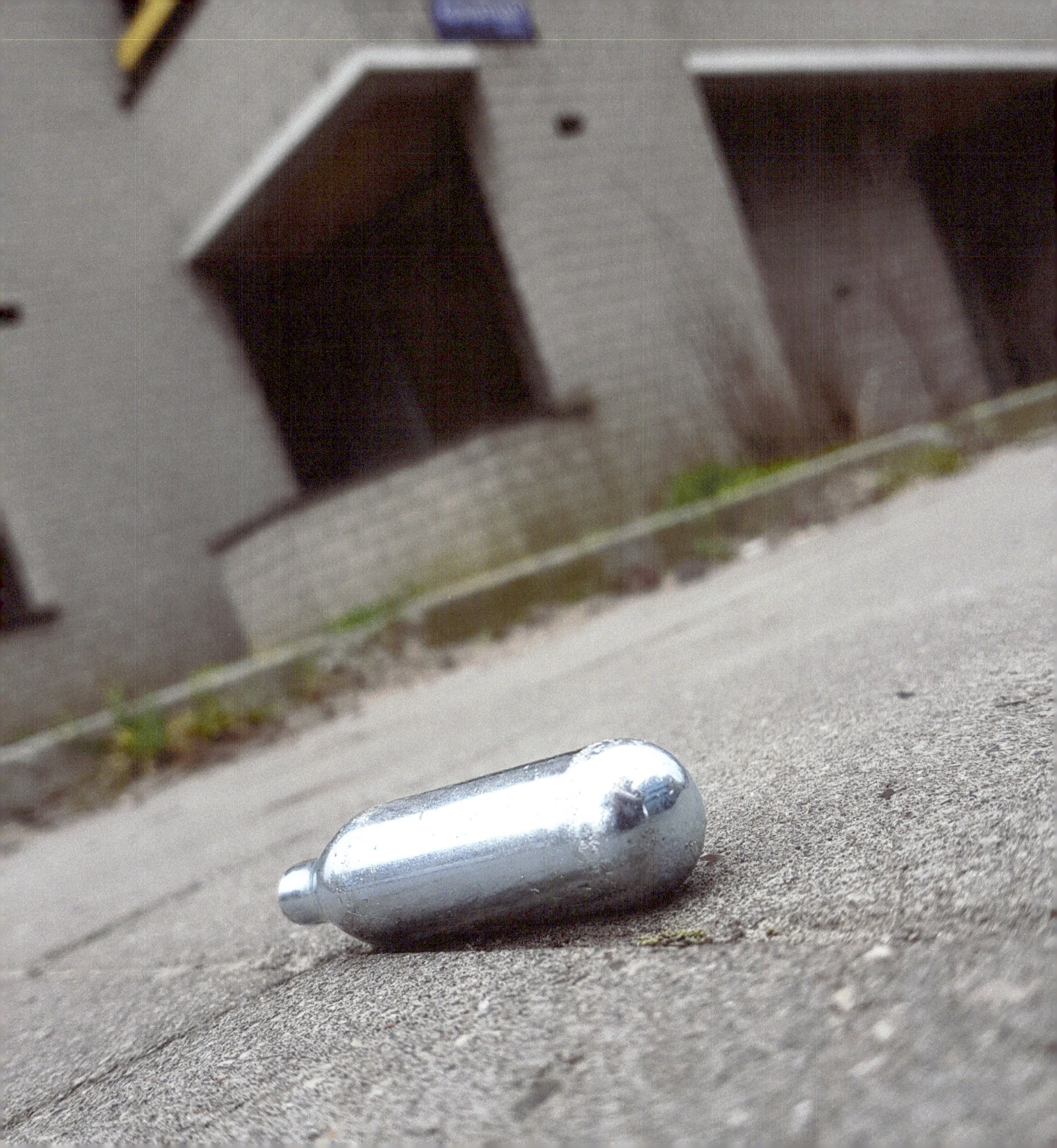

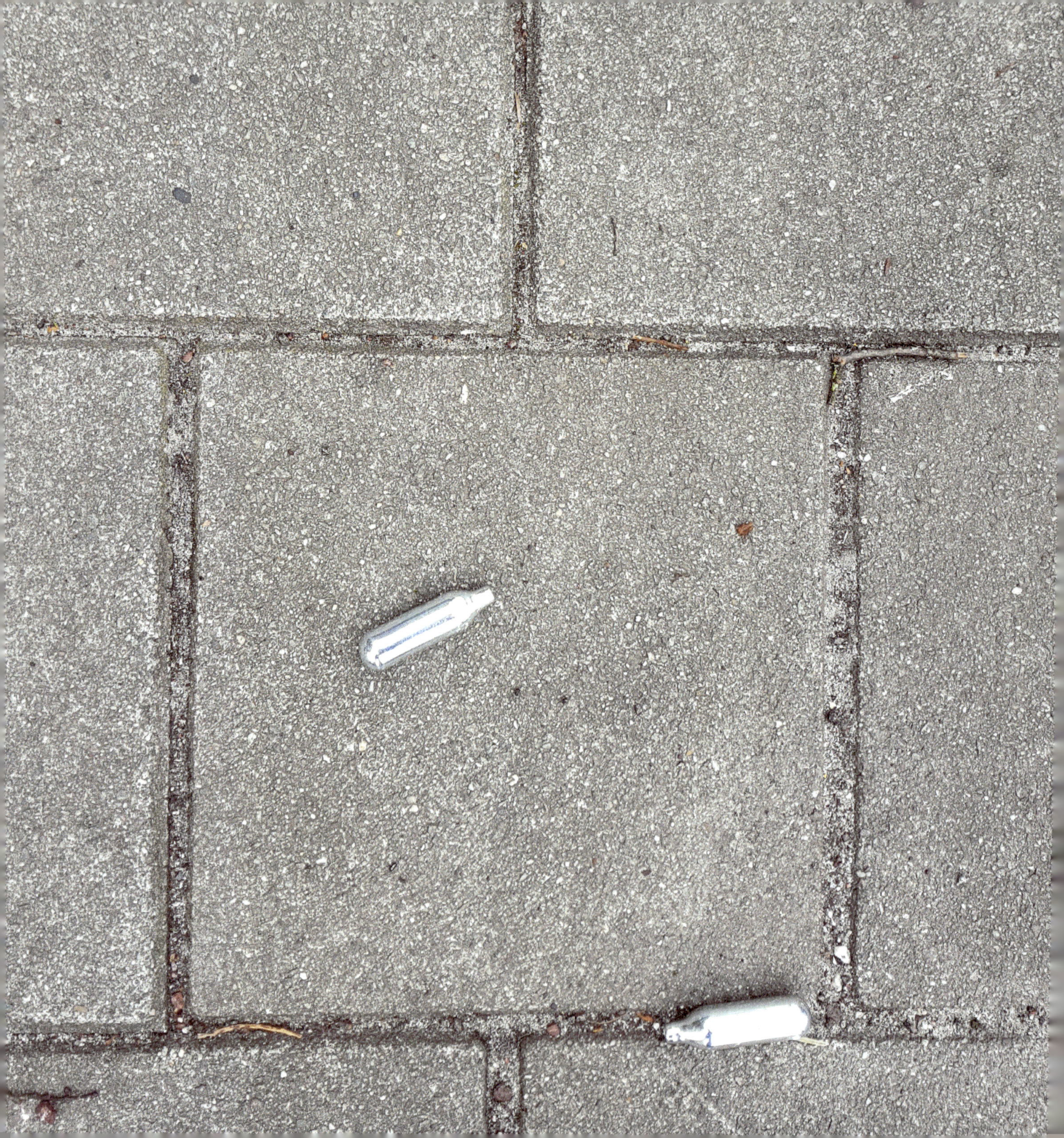

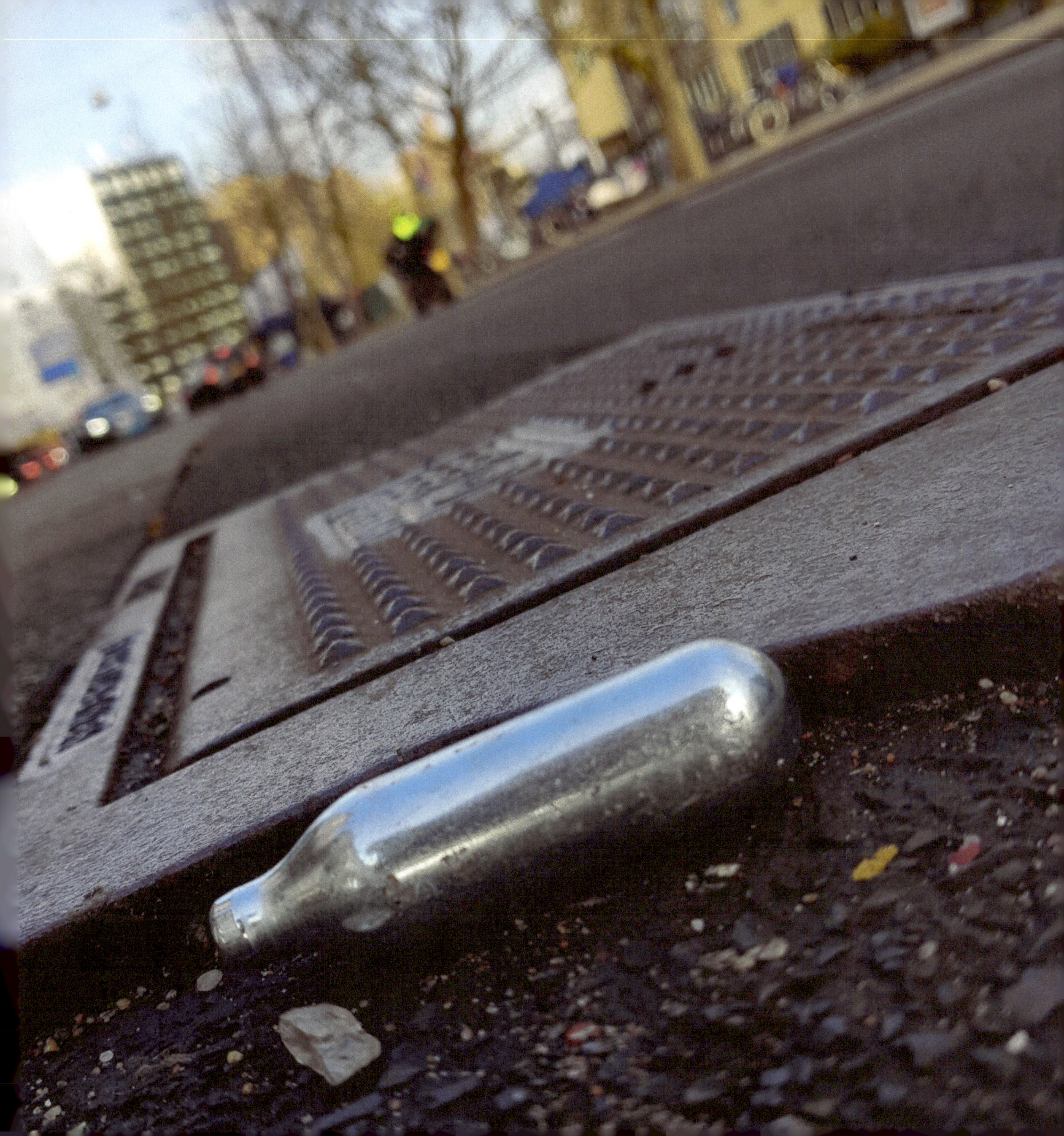

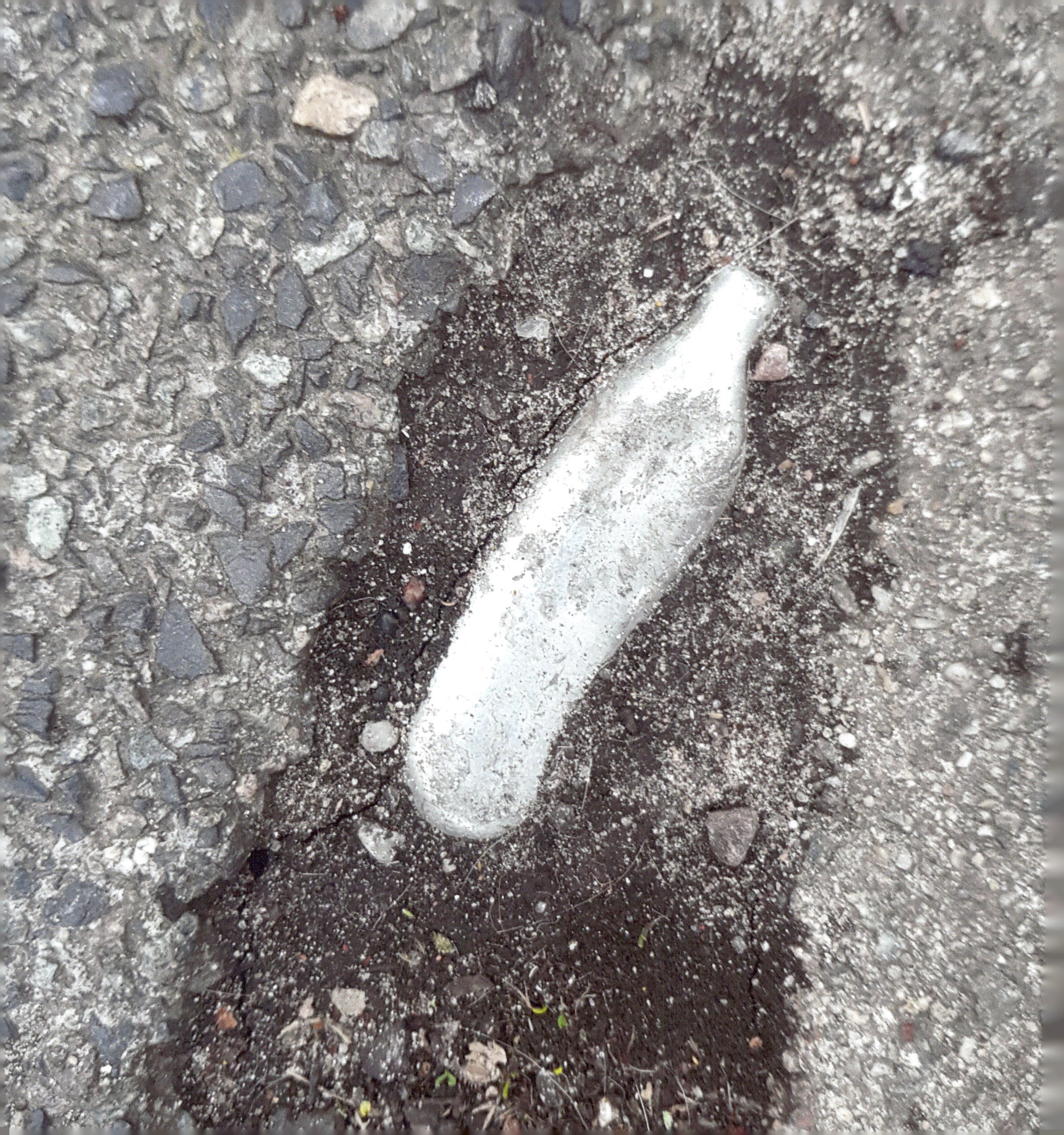

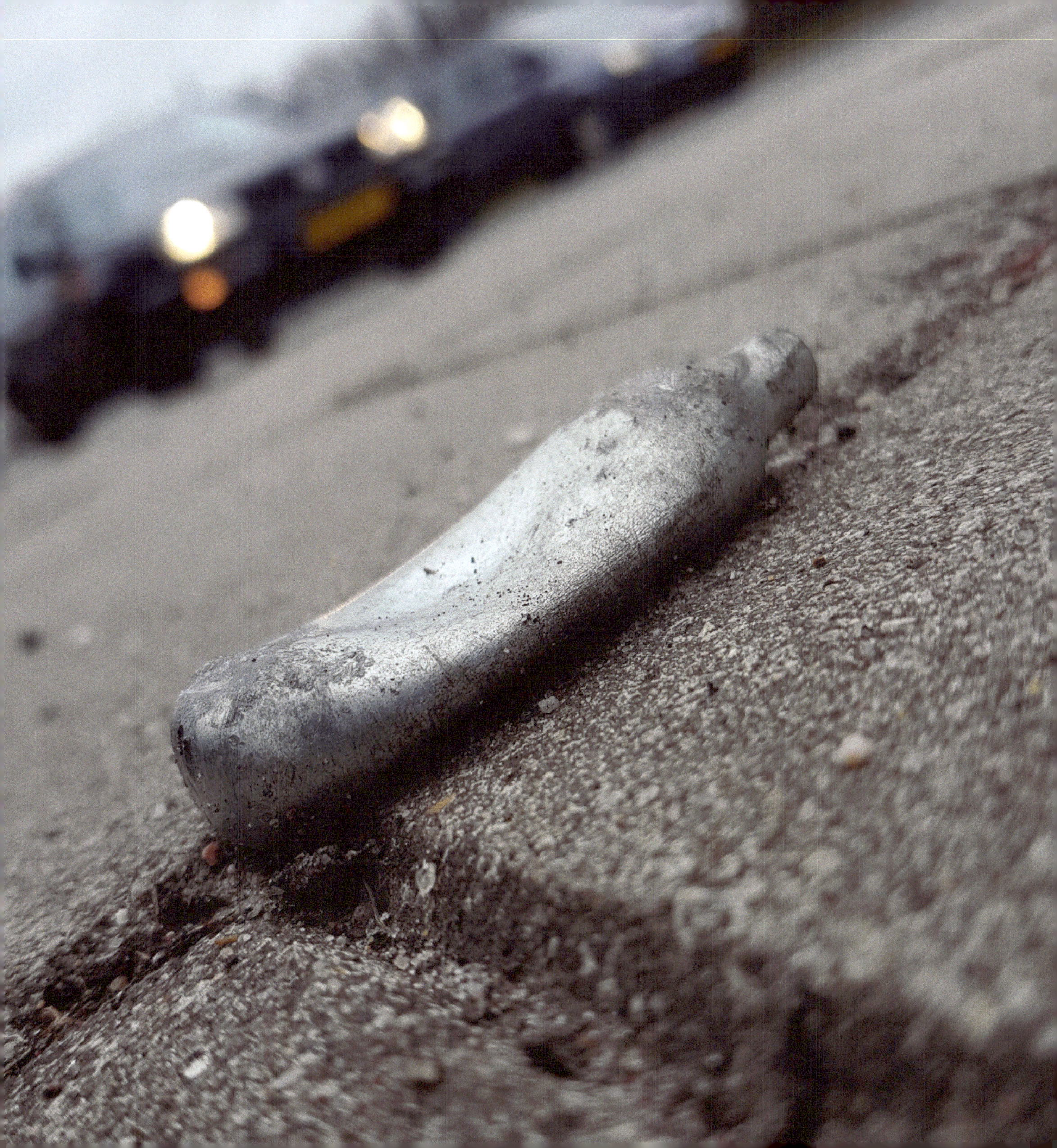

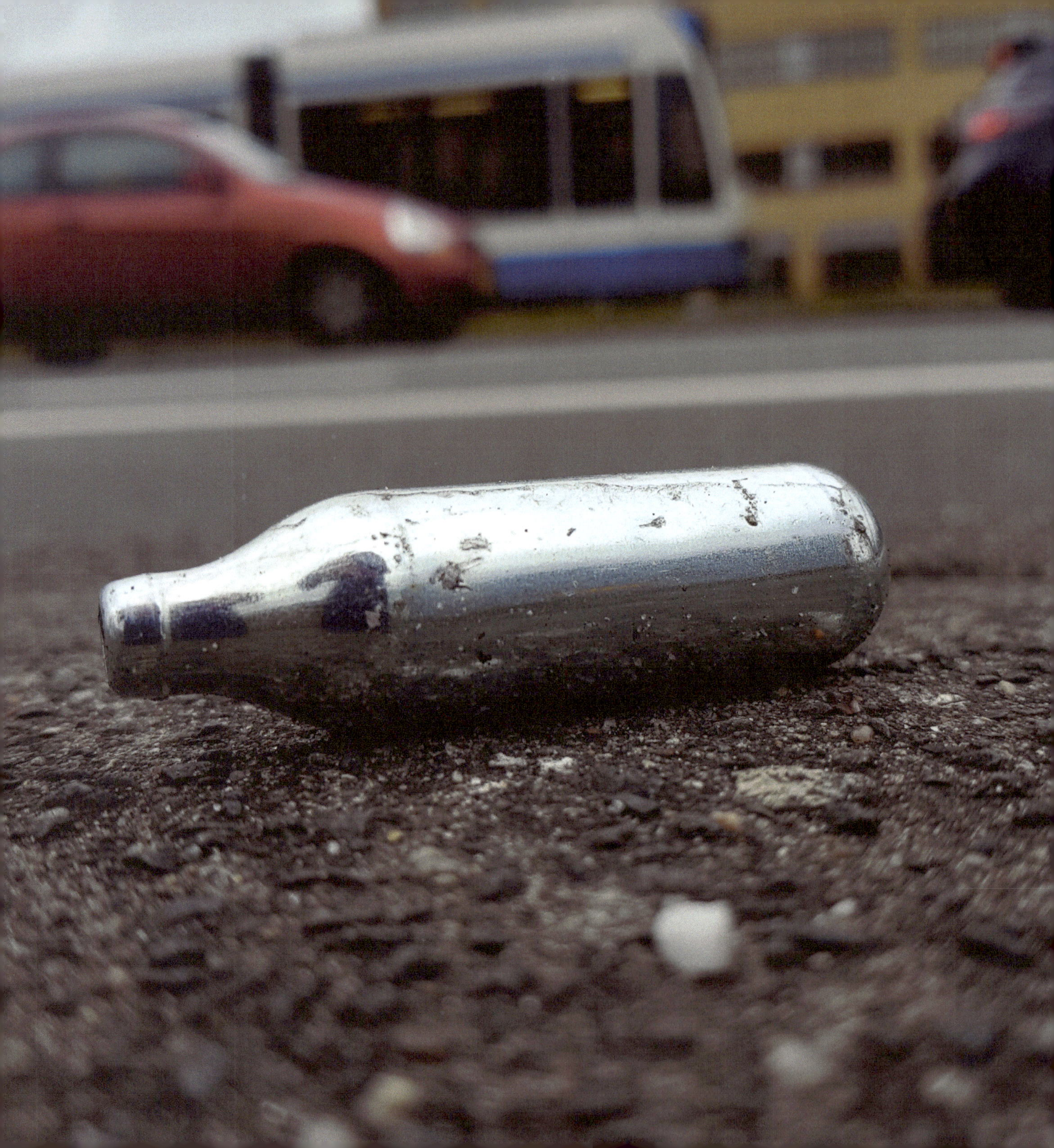

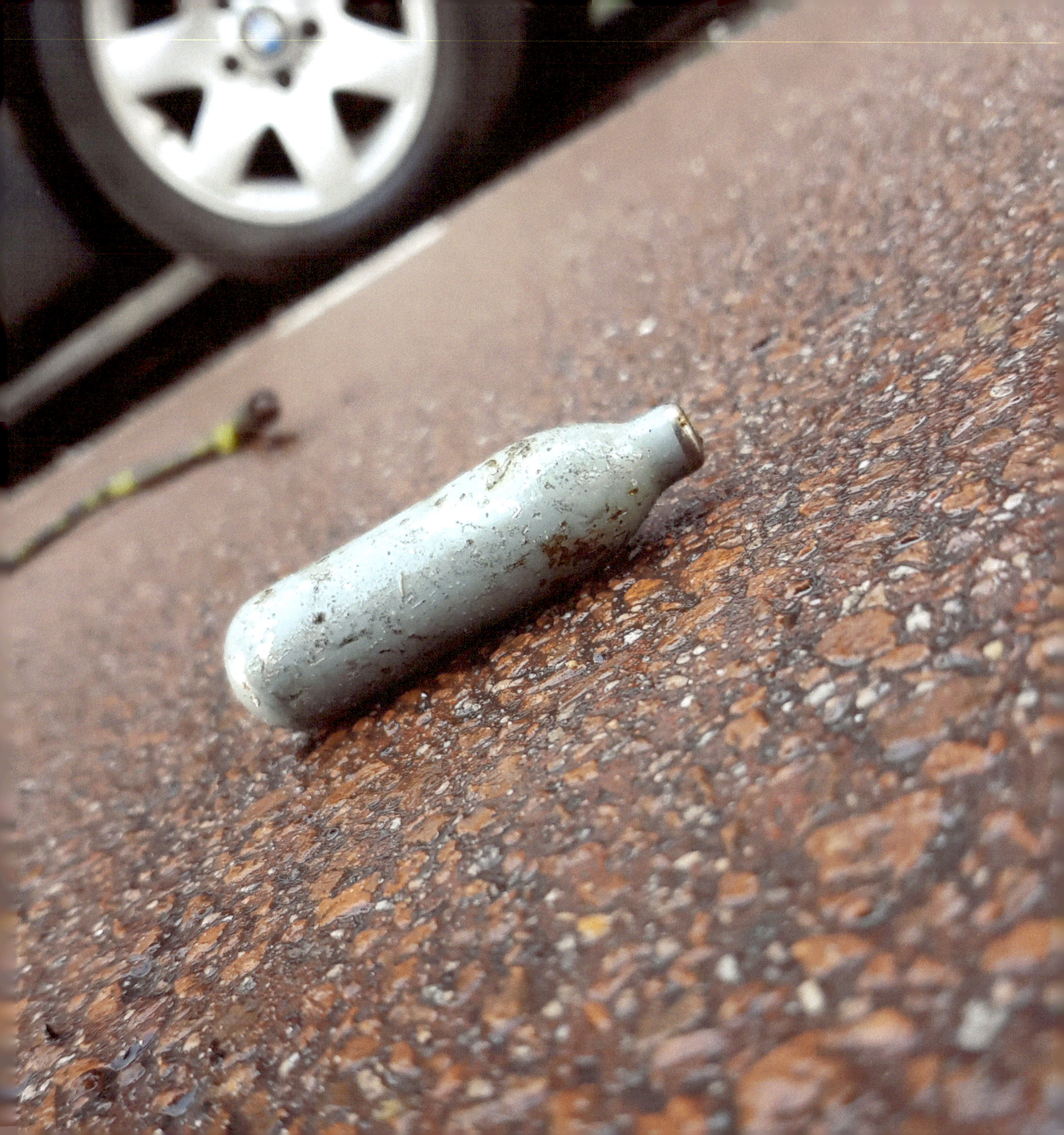

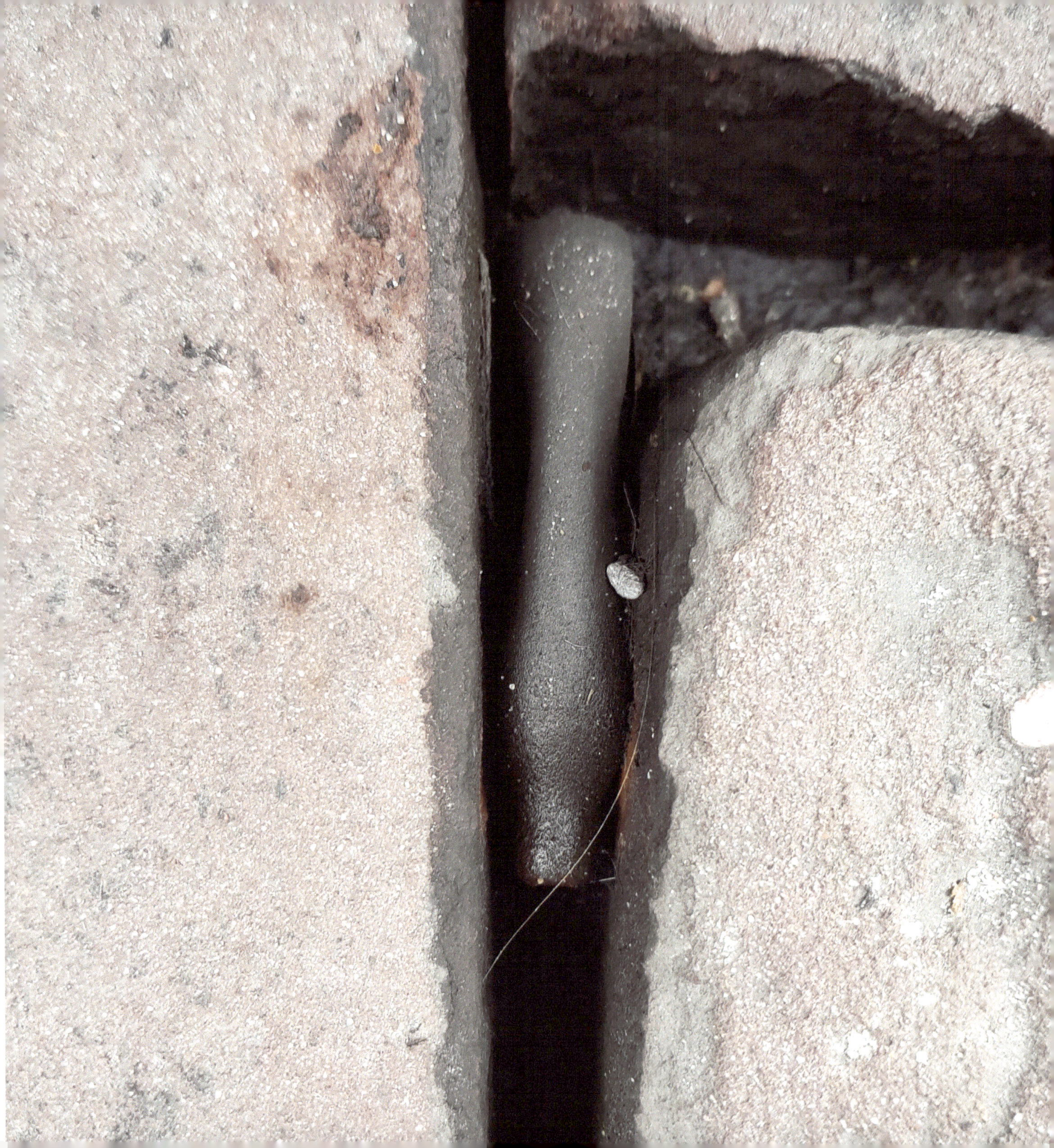

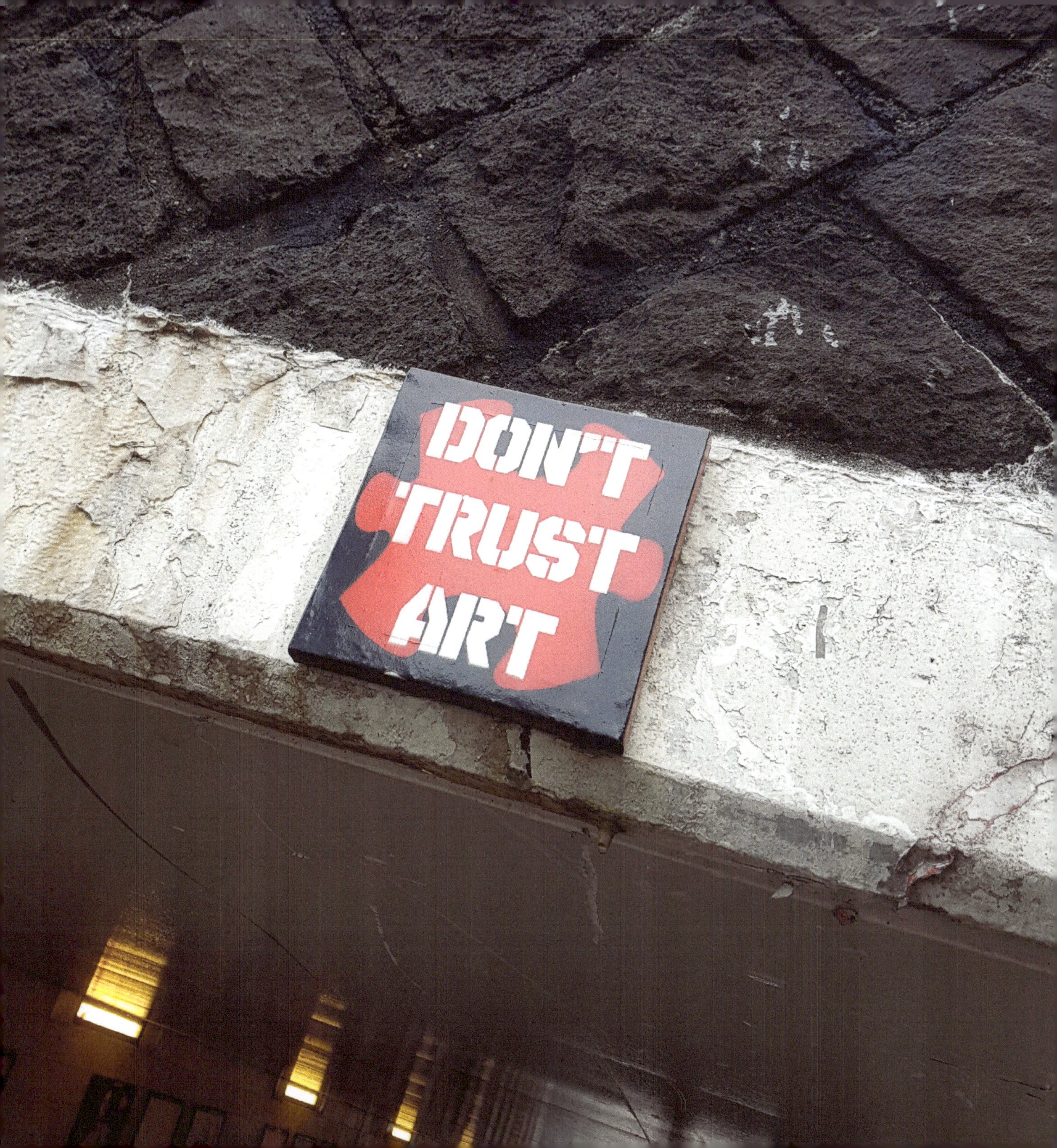
DON'T
TRUST
ART

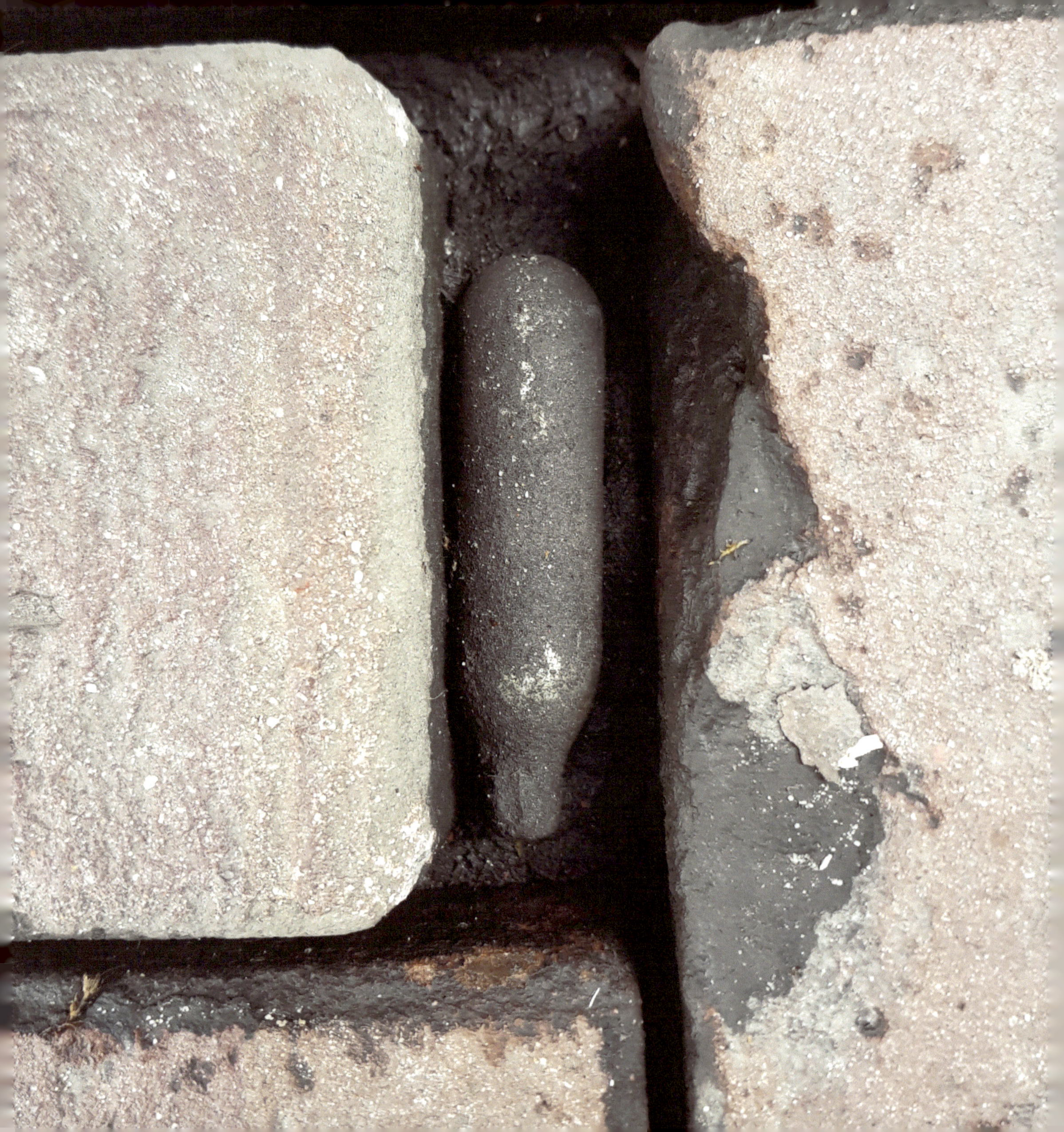

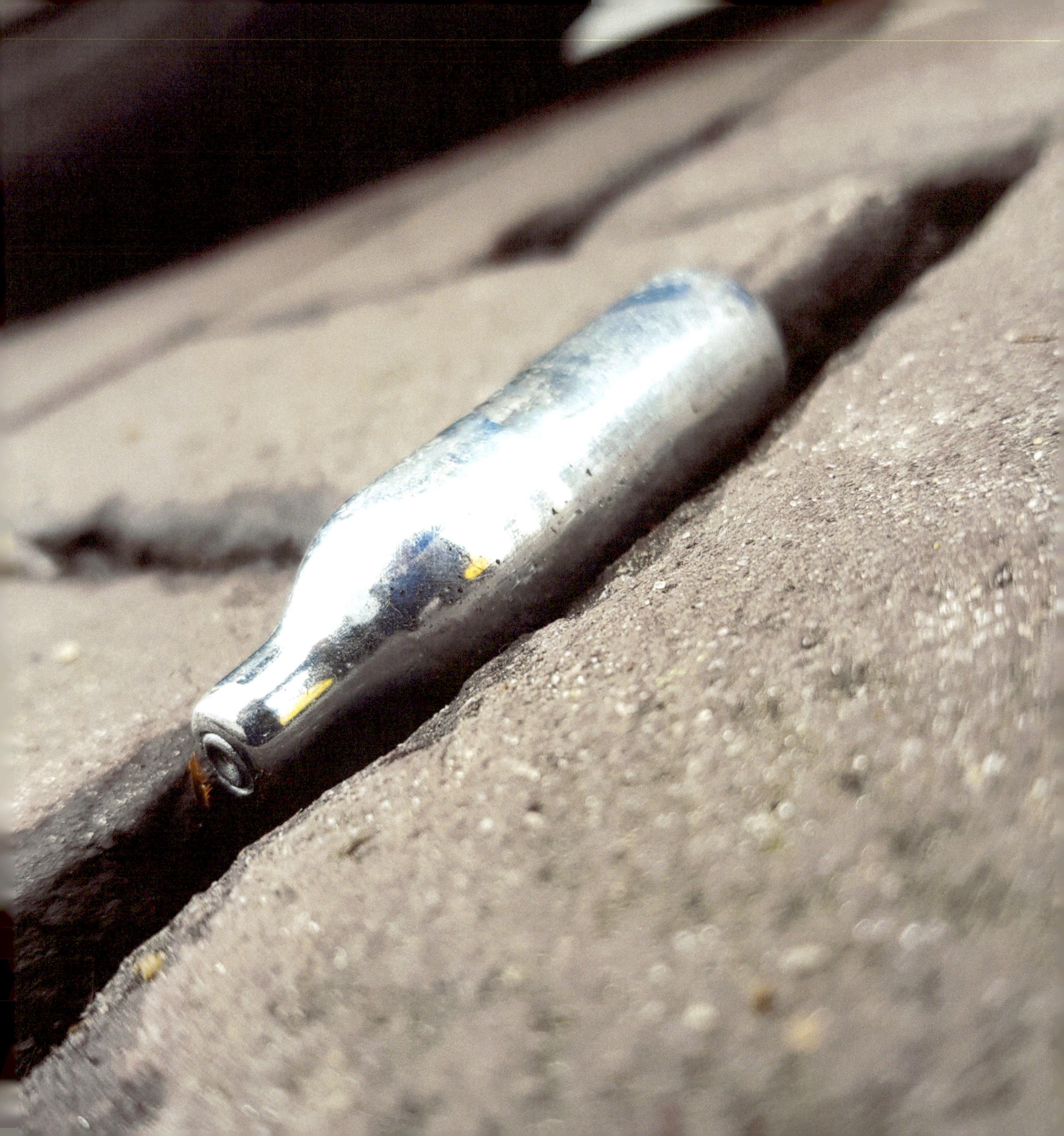

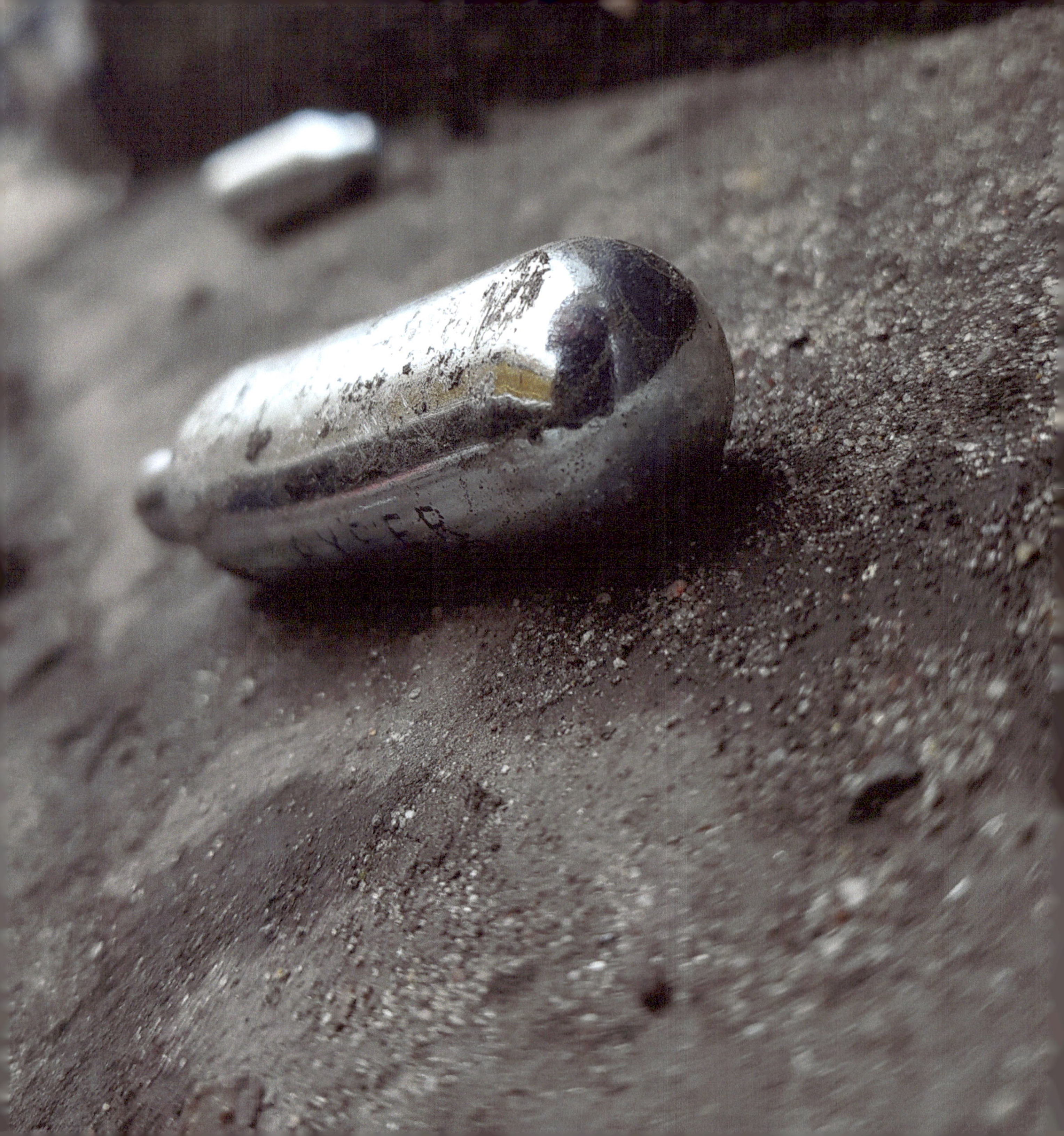

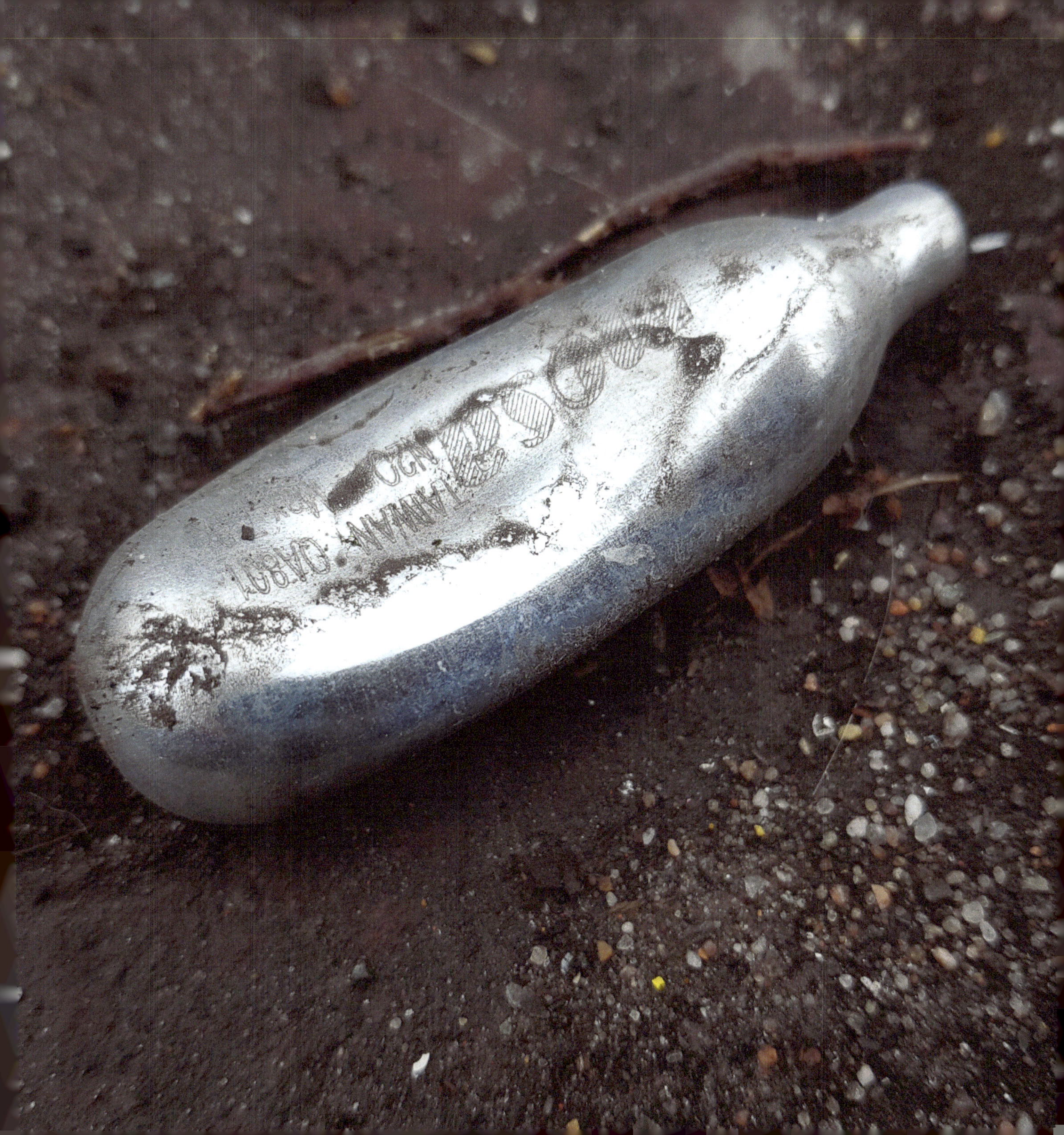

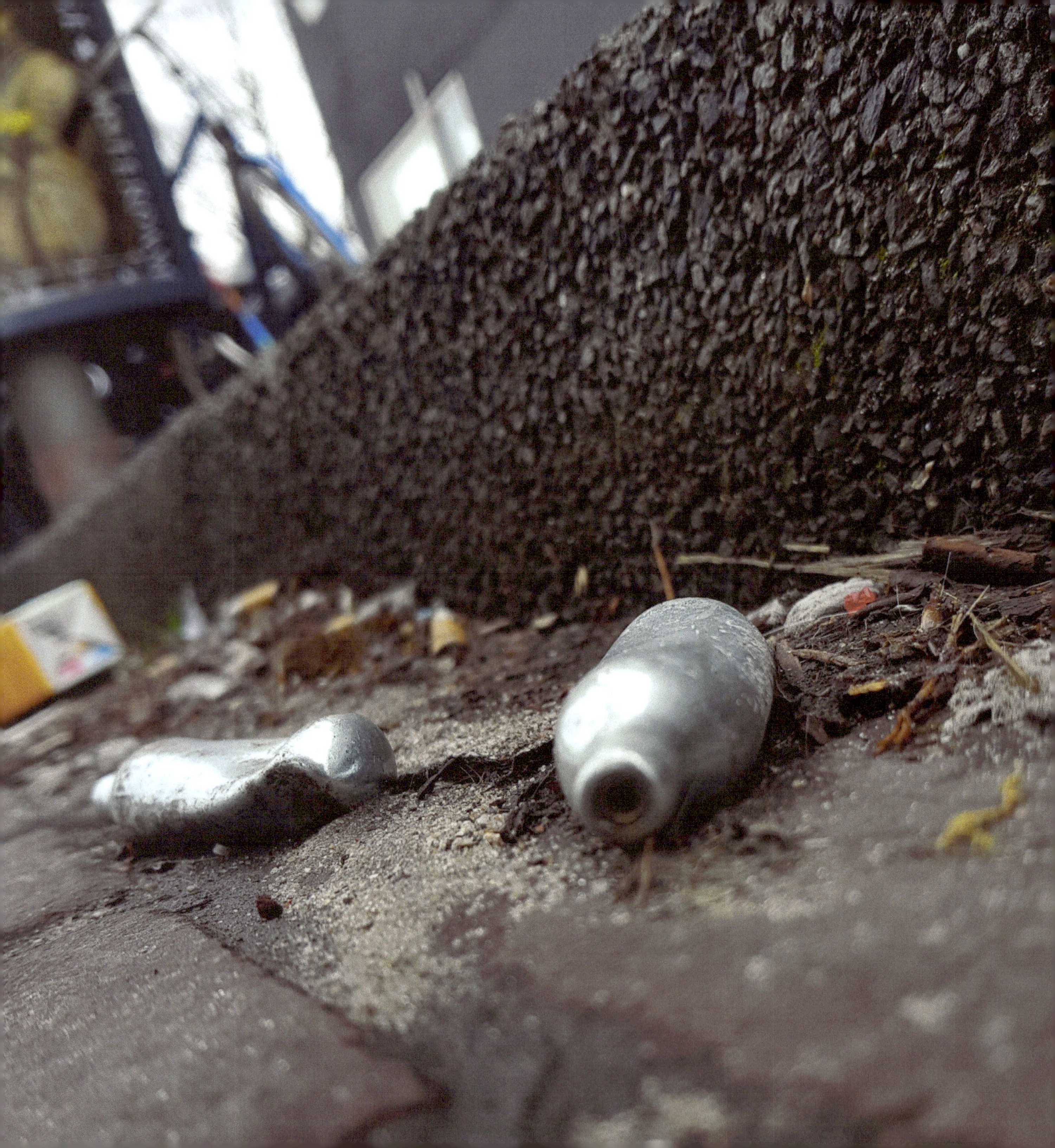

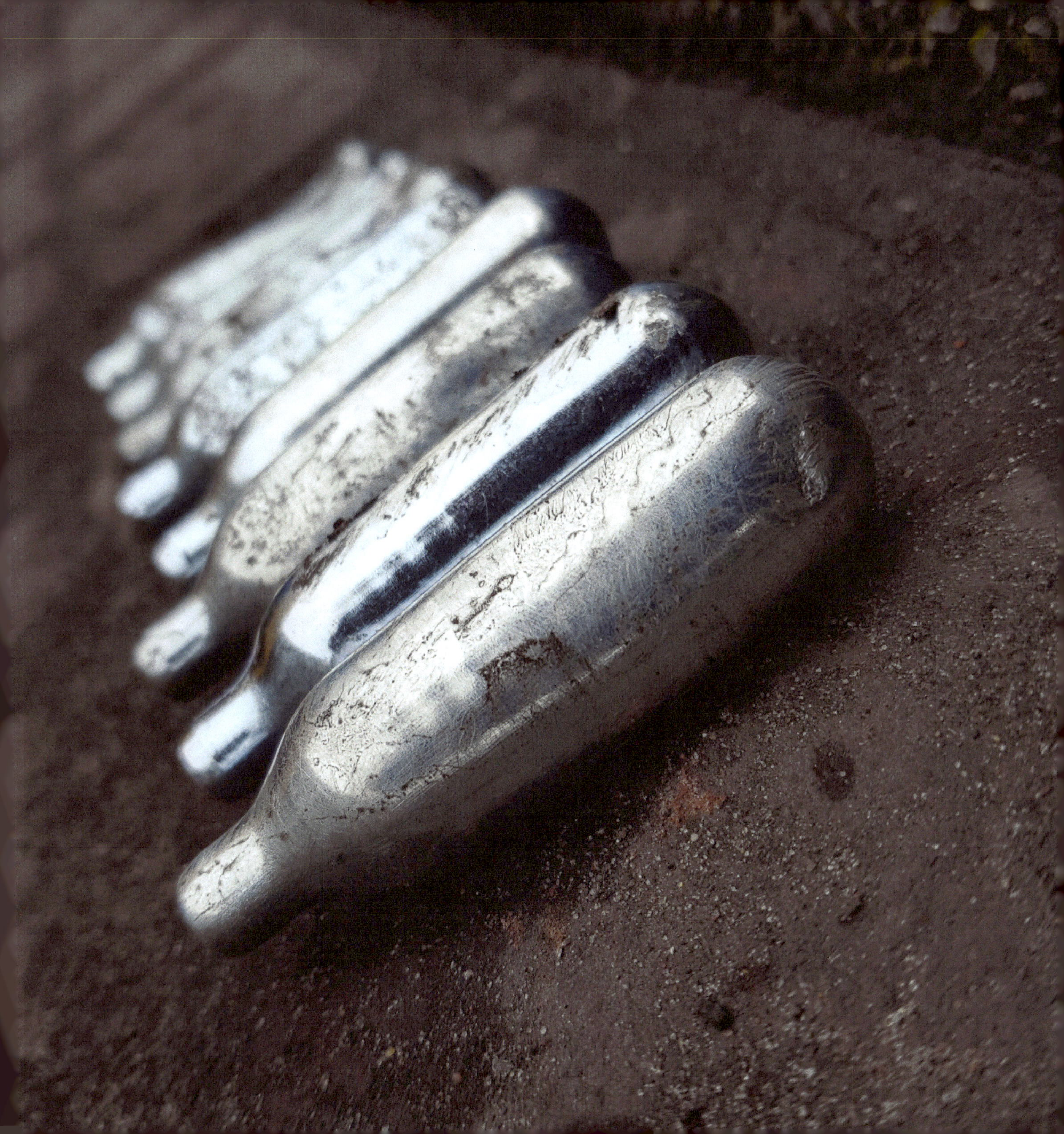

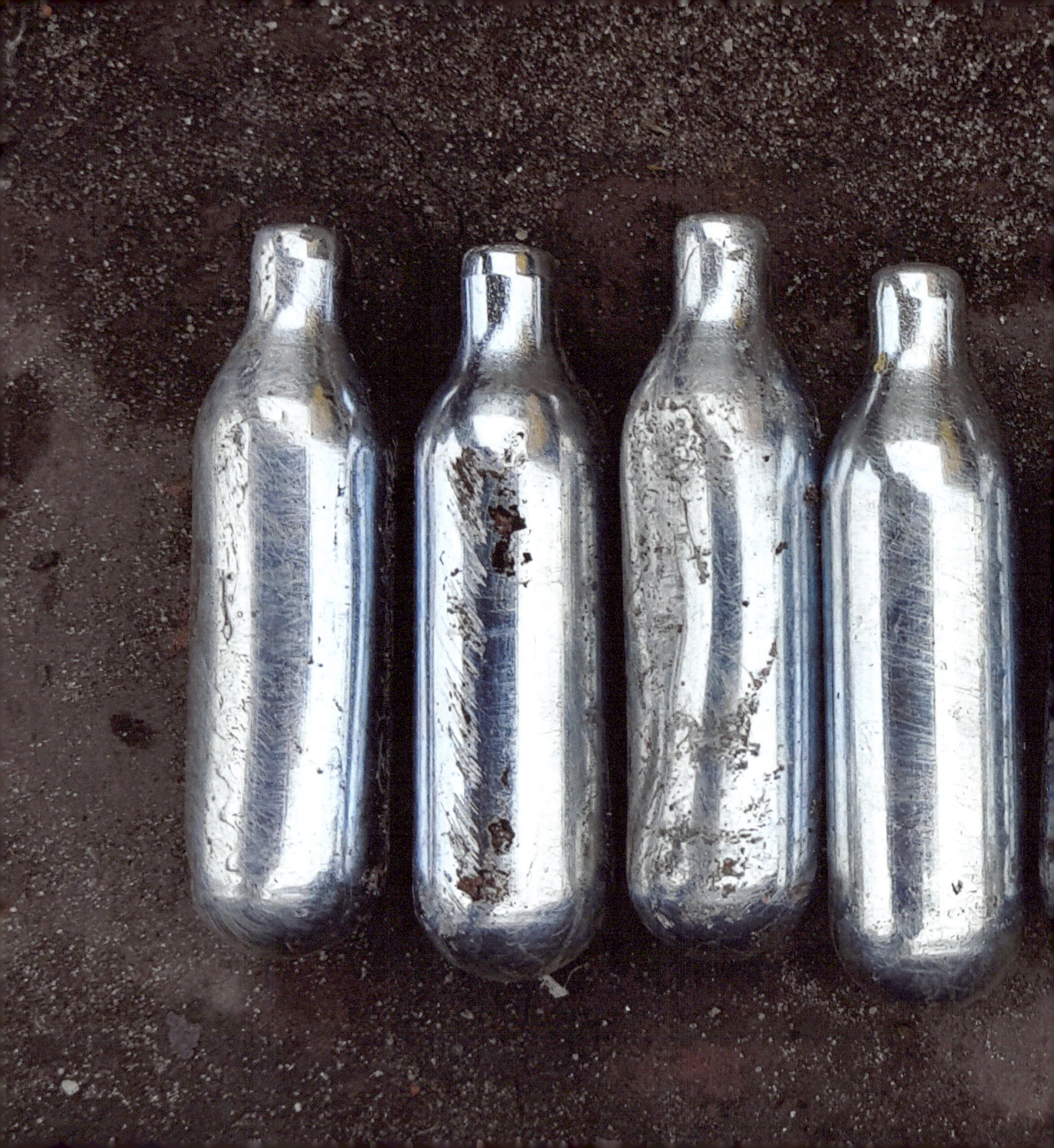

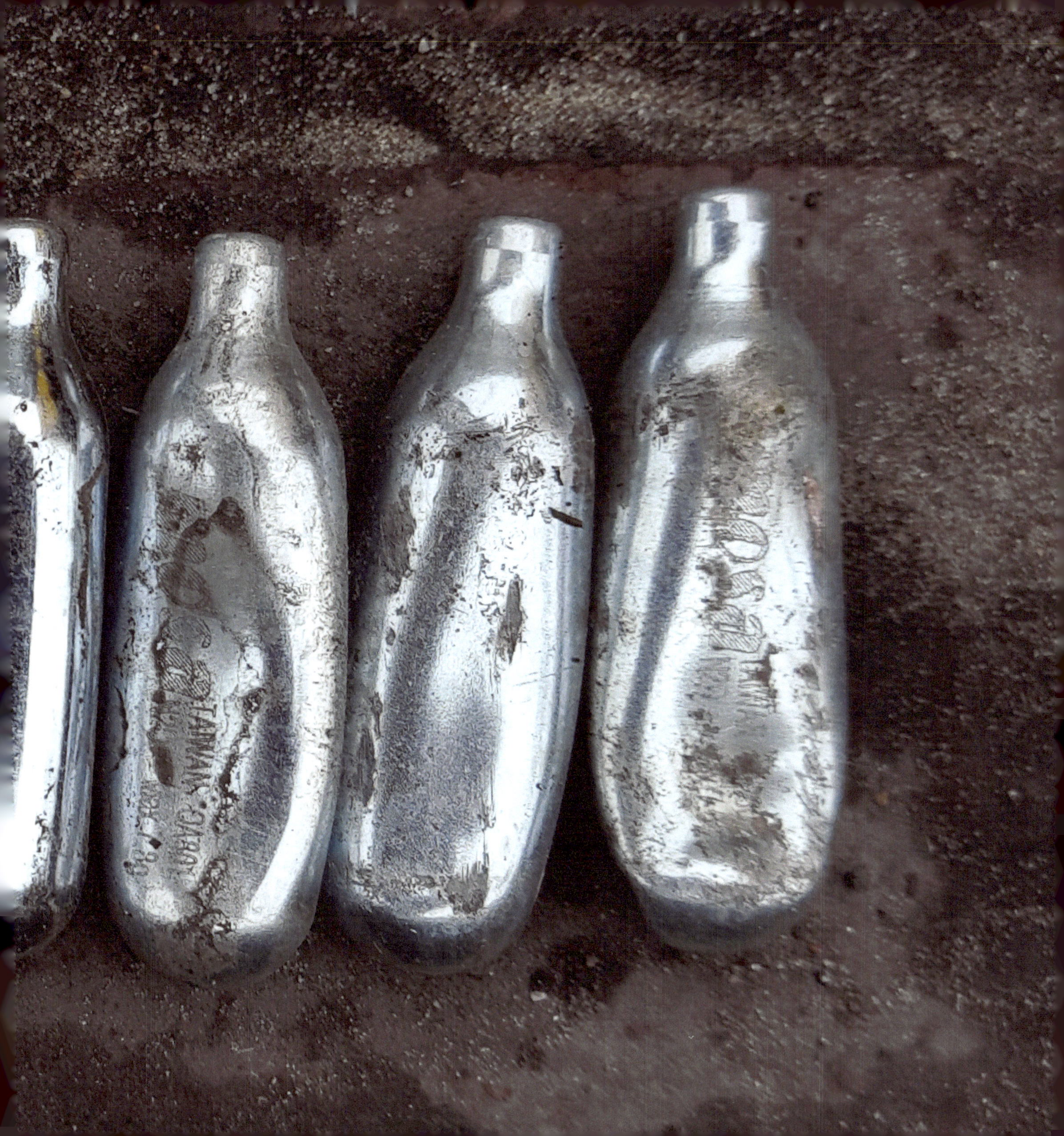

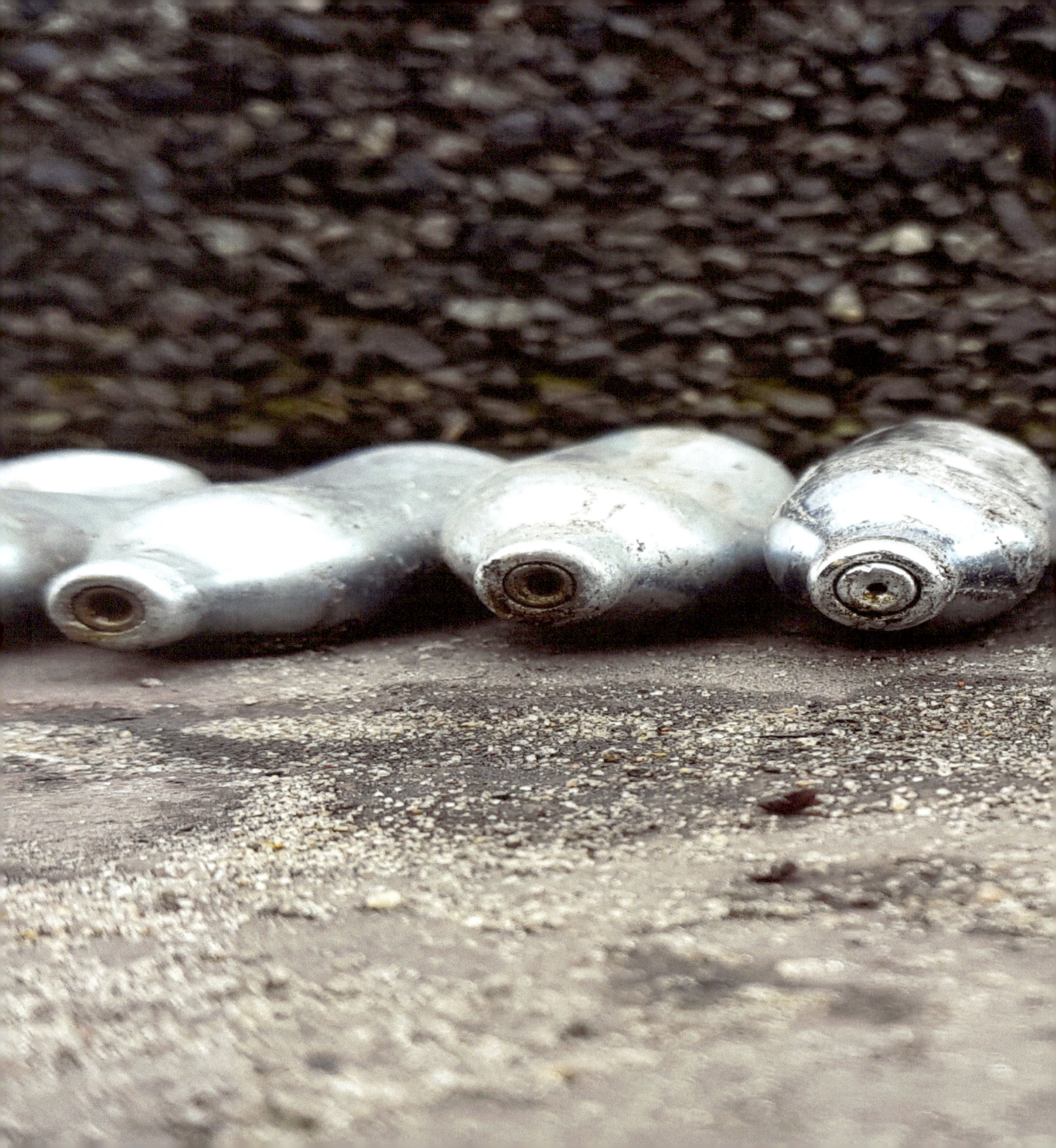

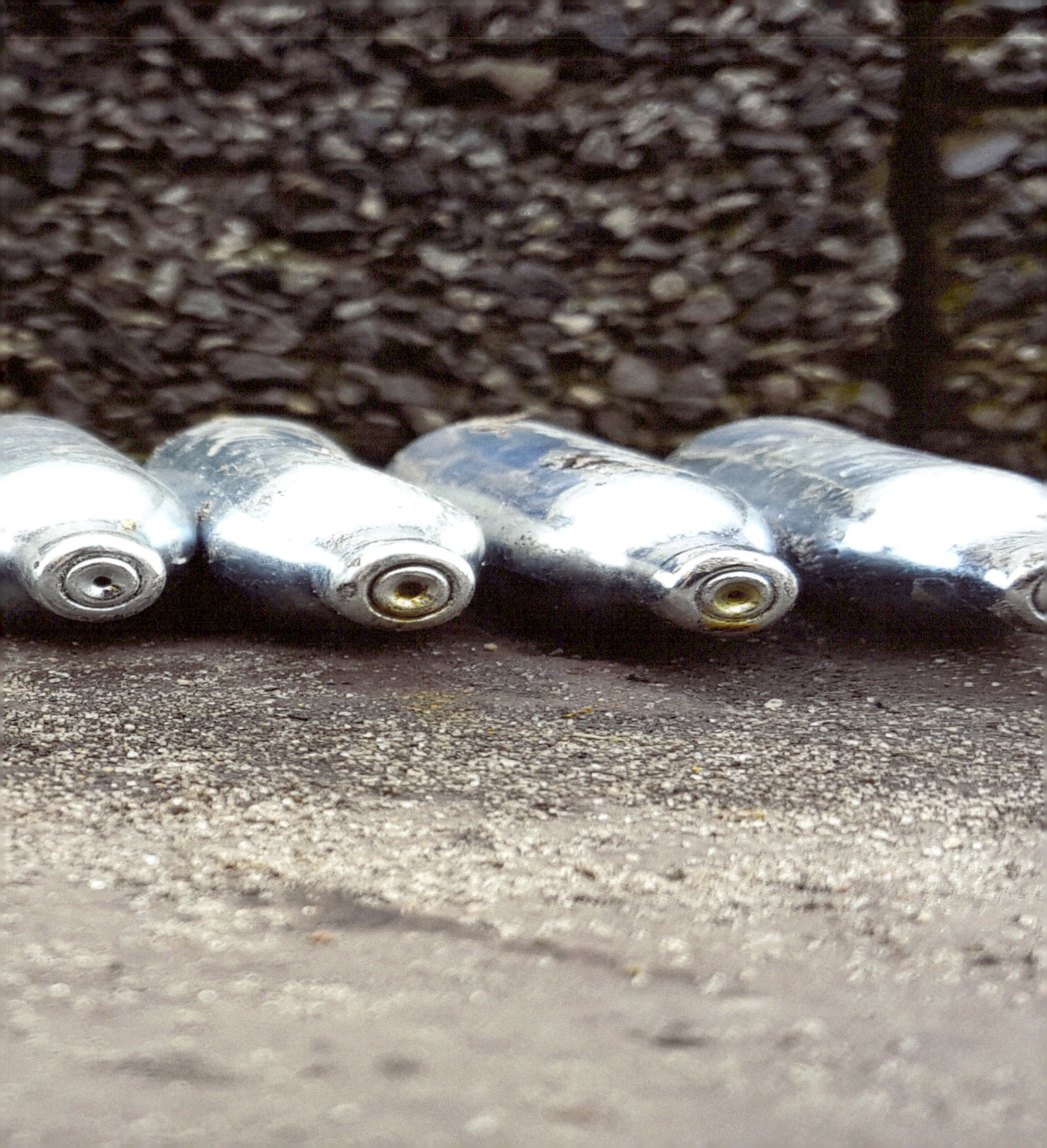

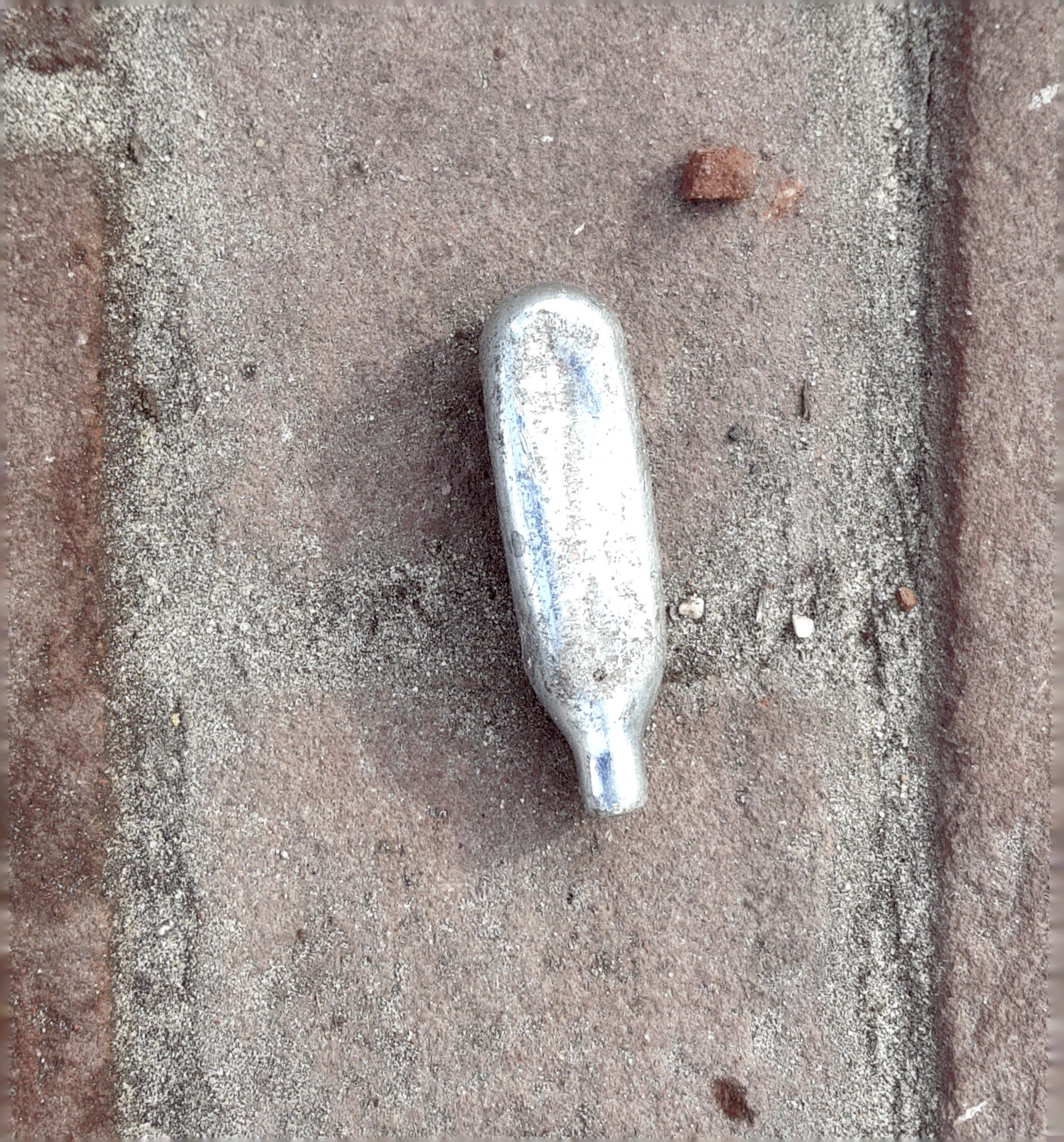

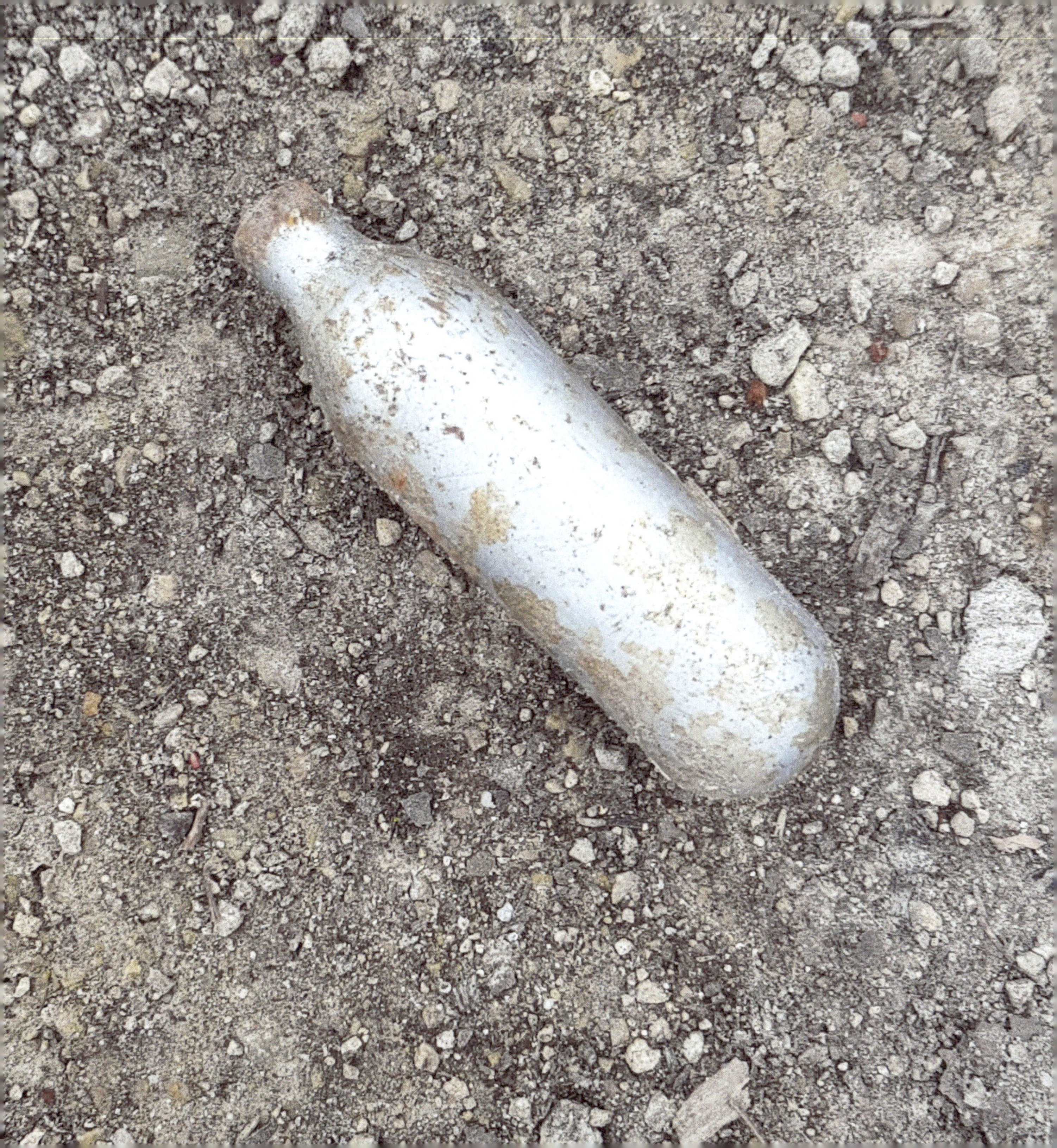

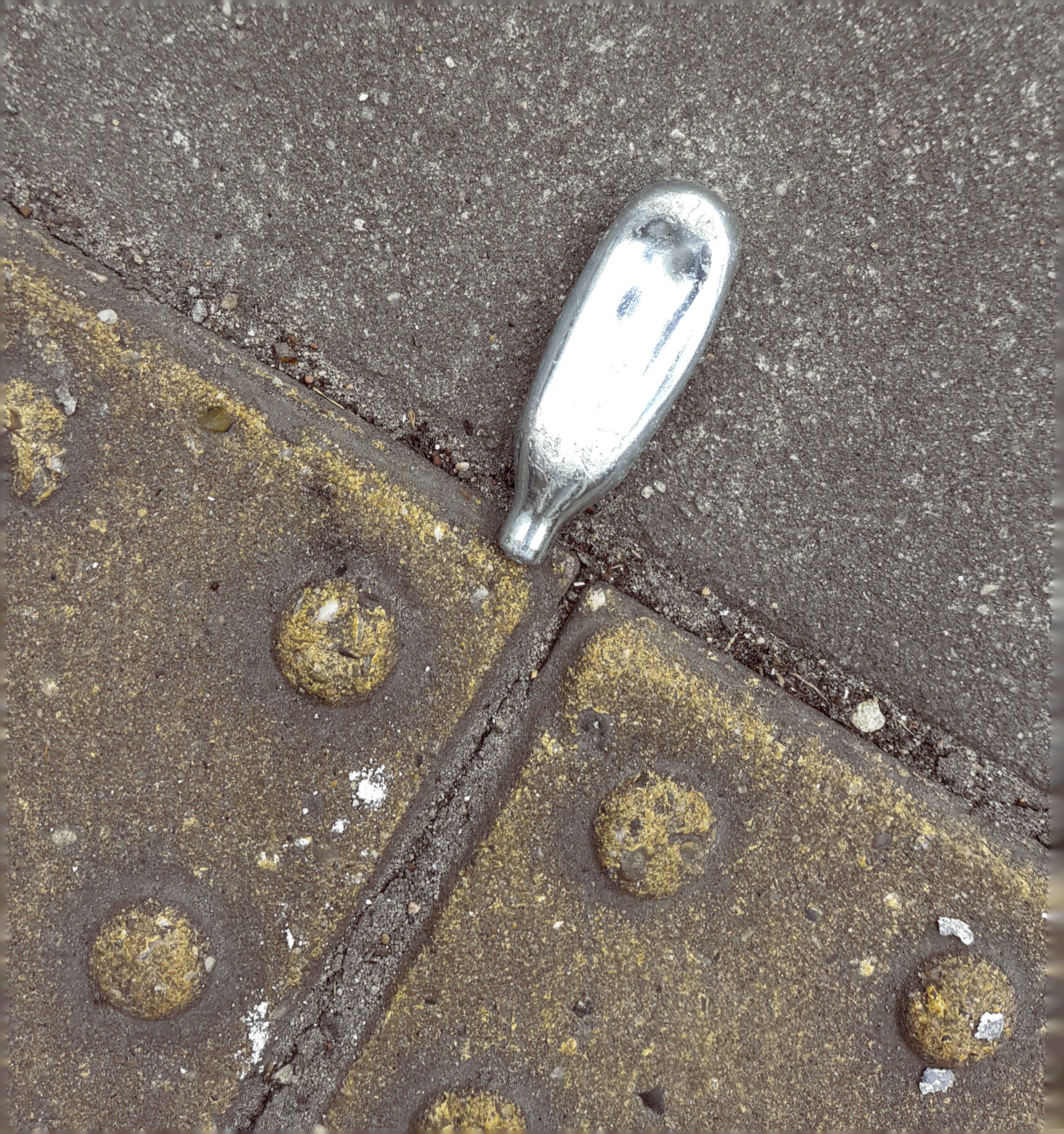

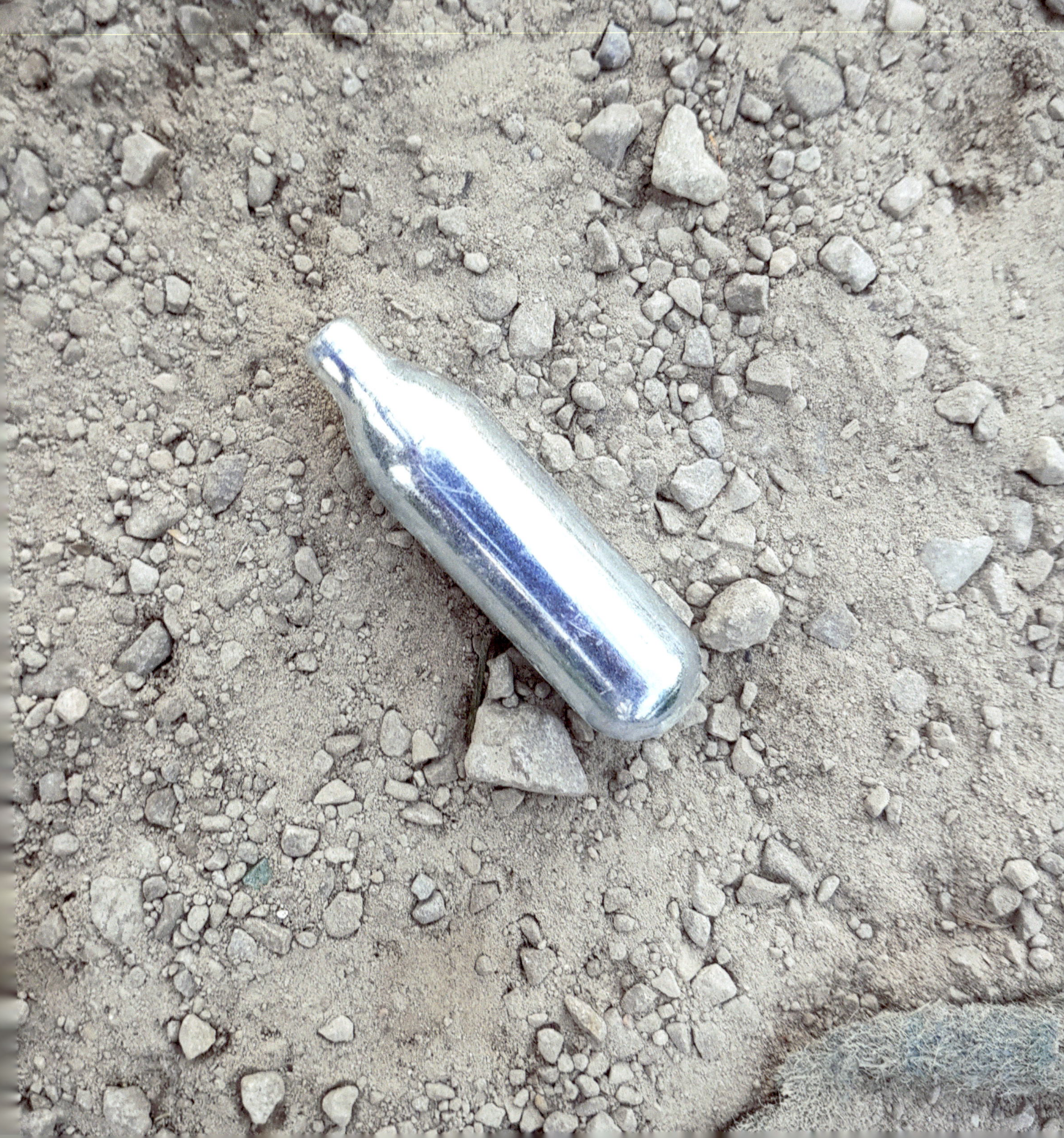

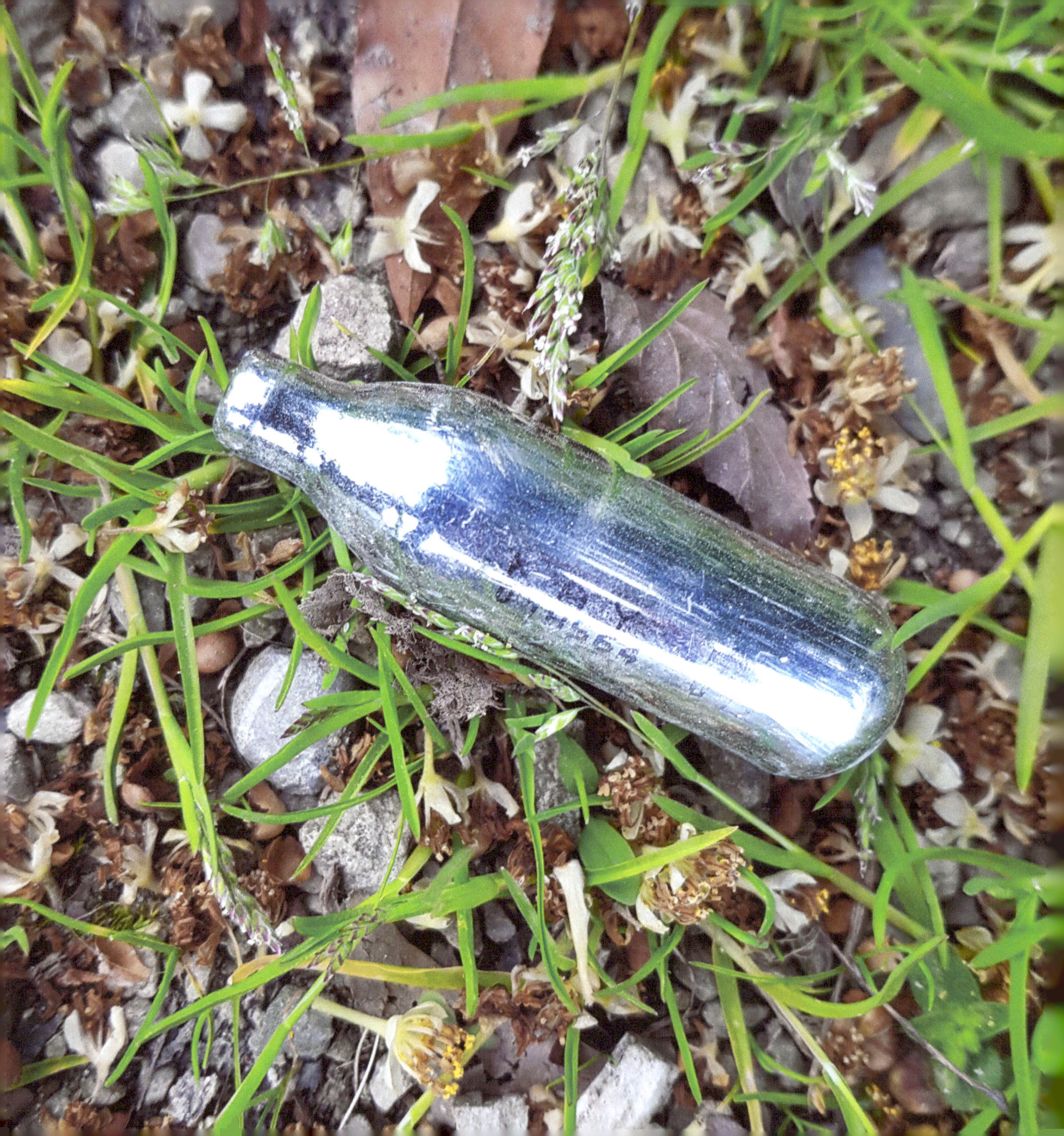

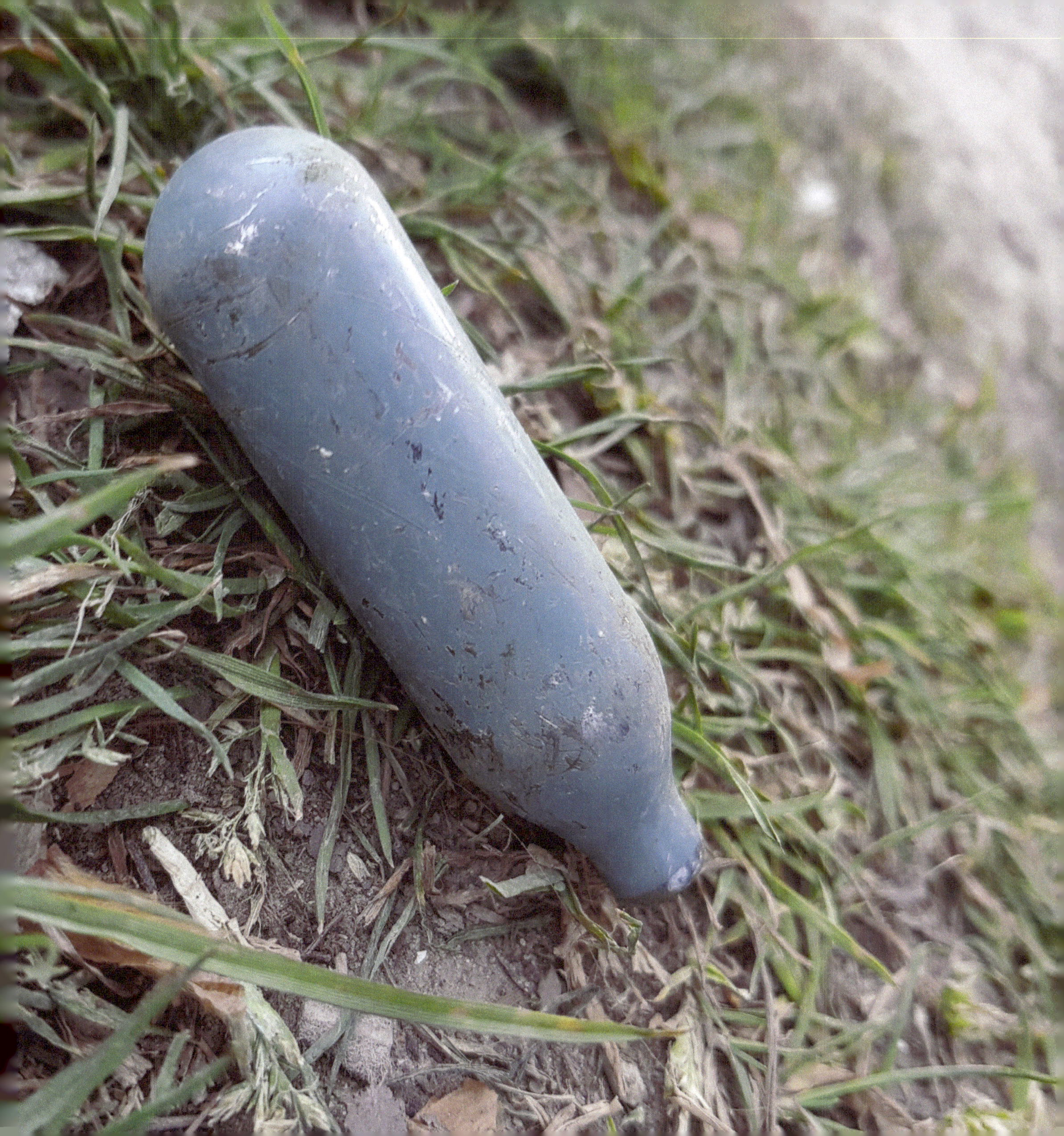

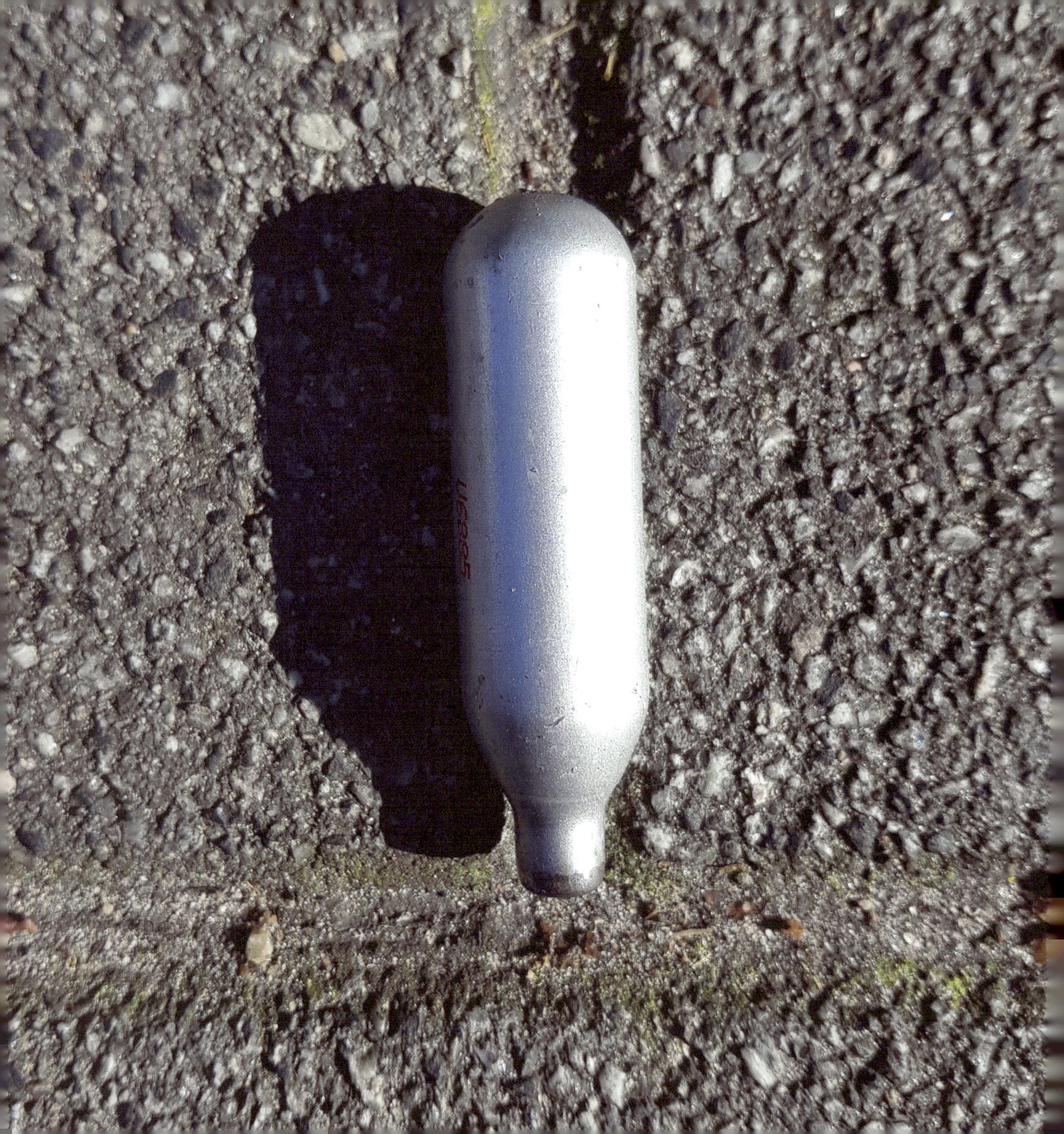

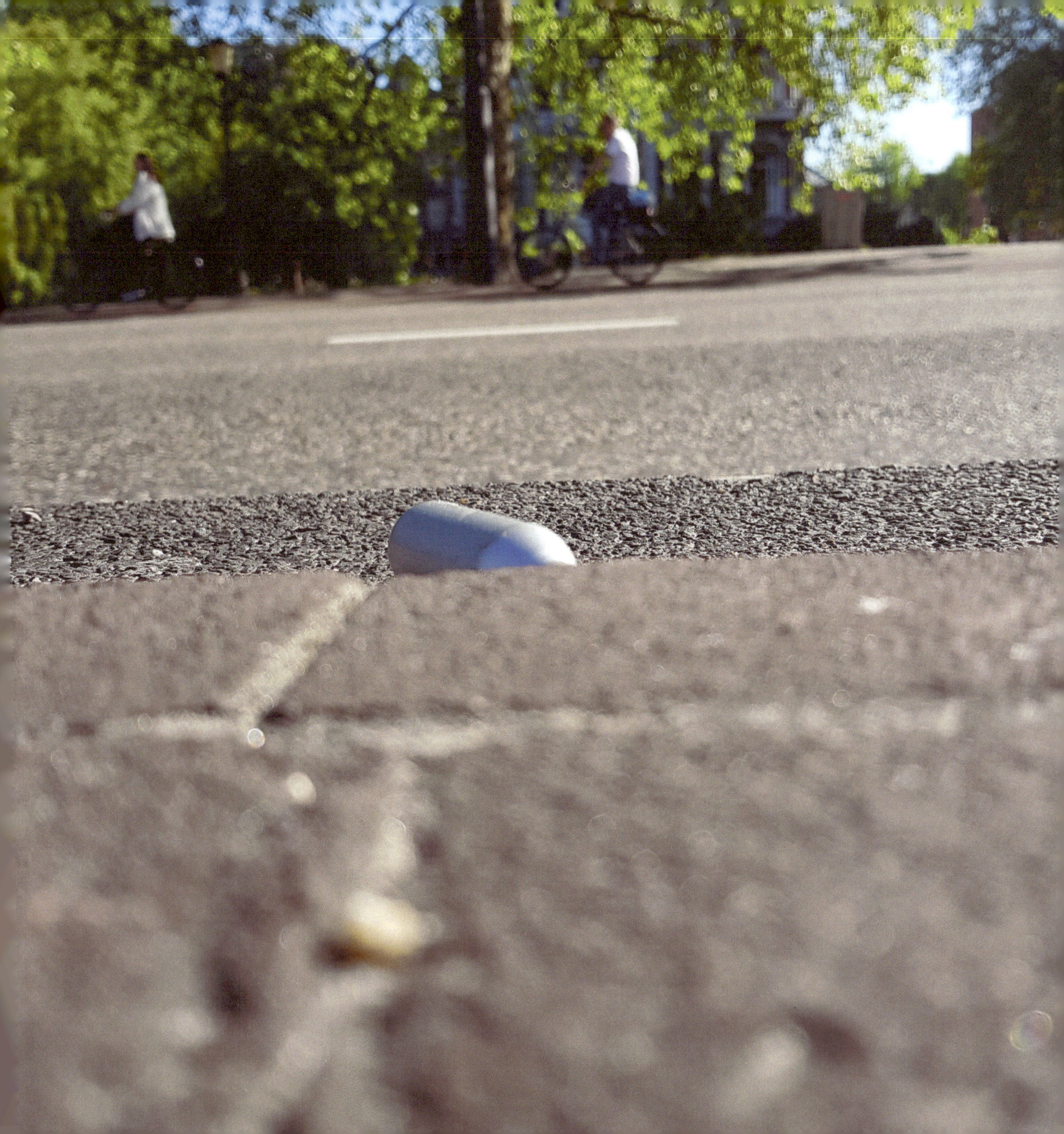

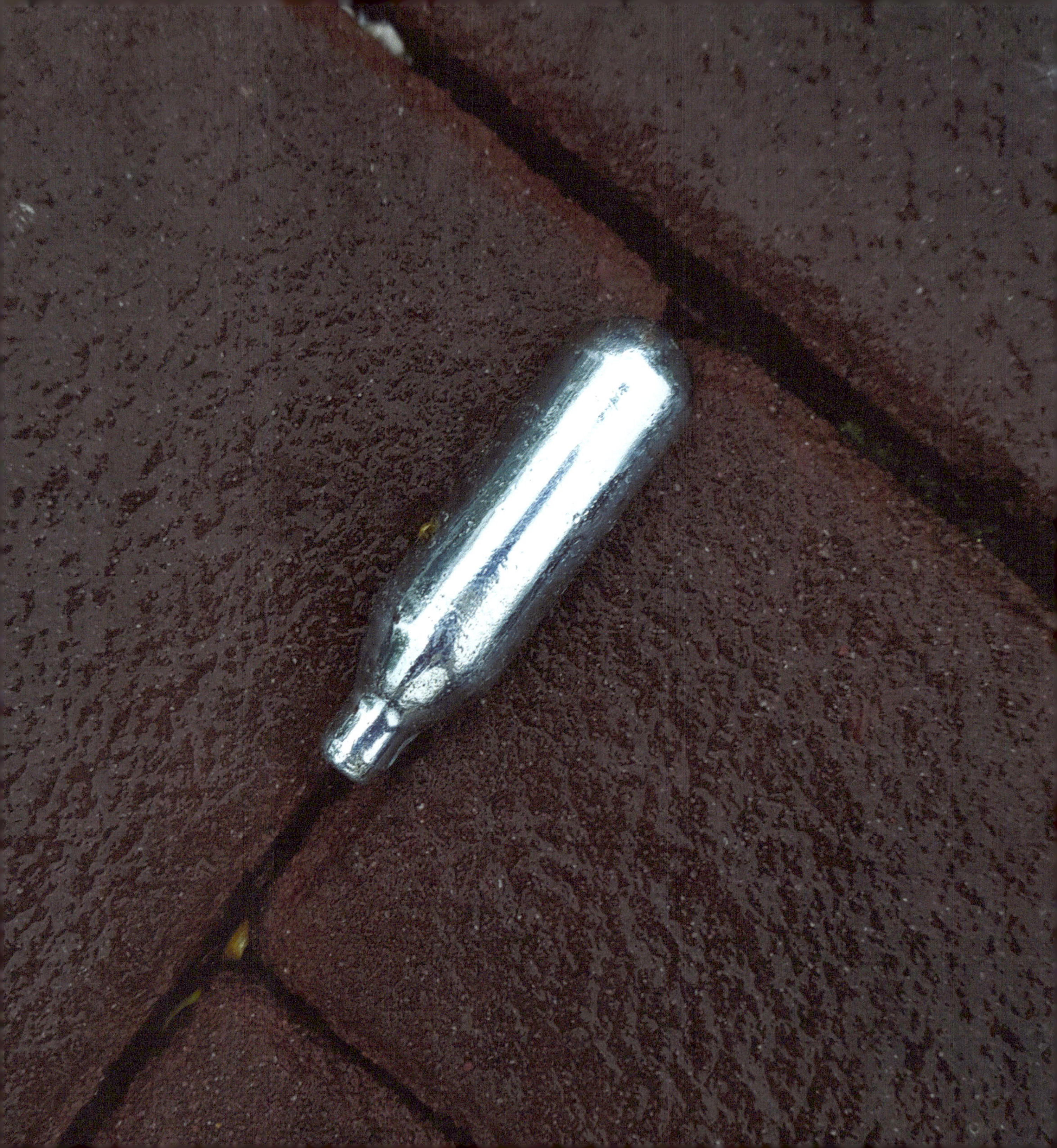

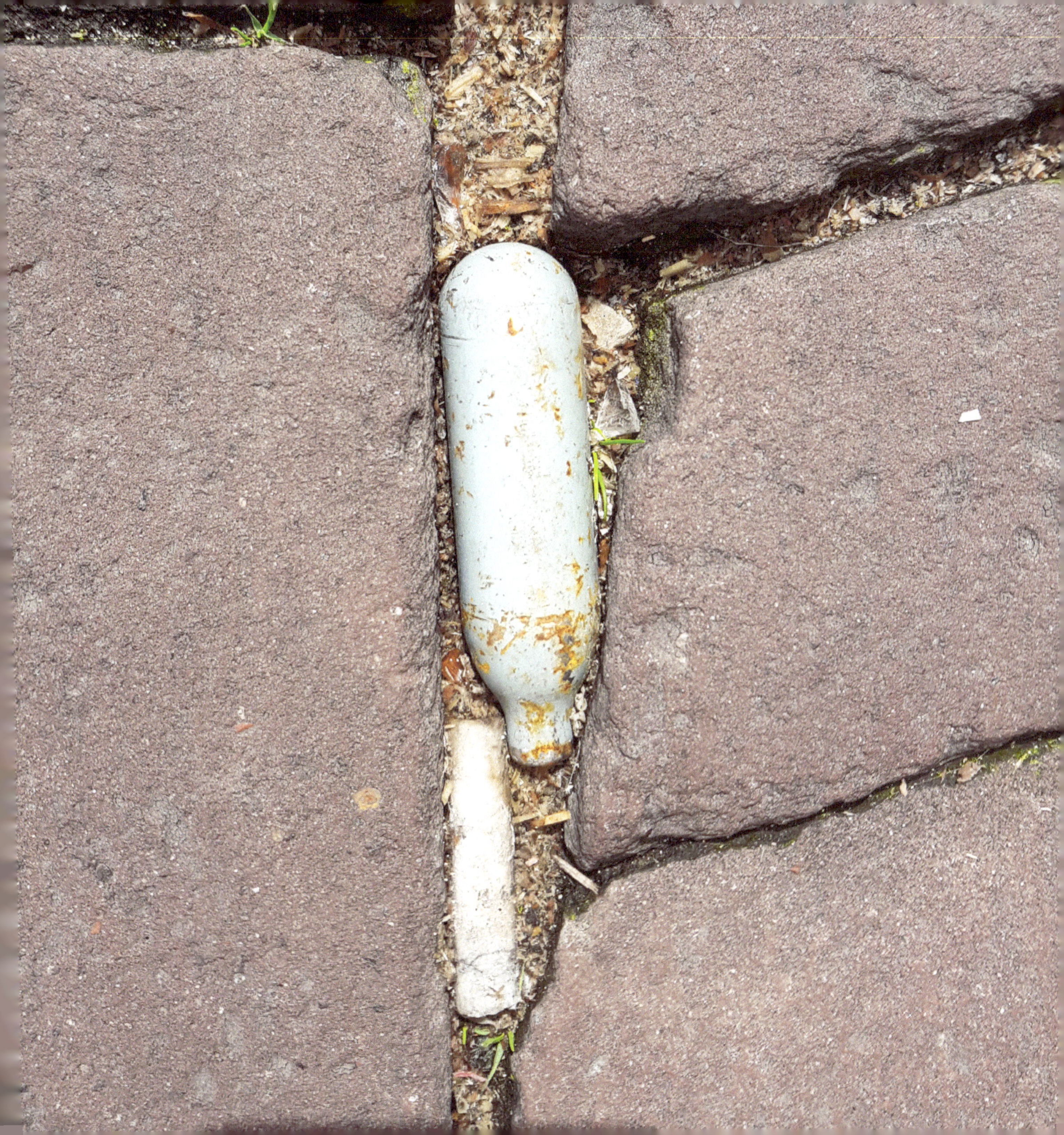

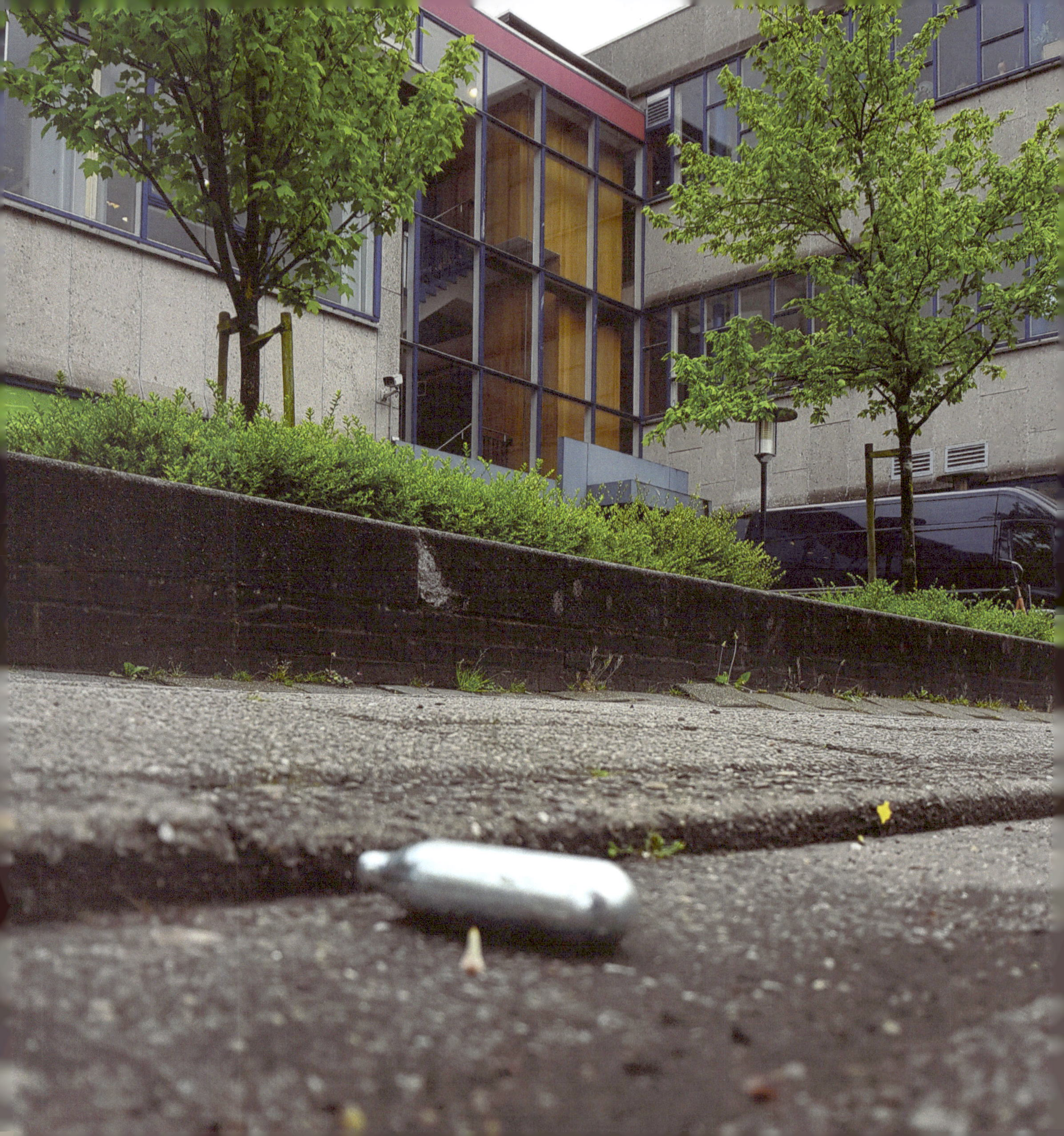

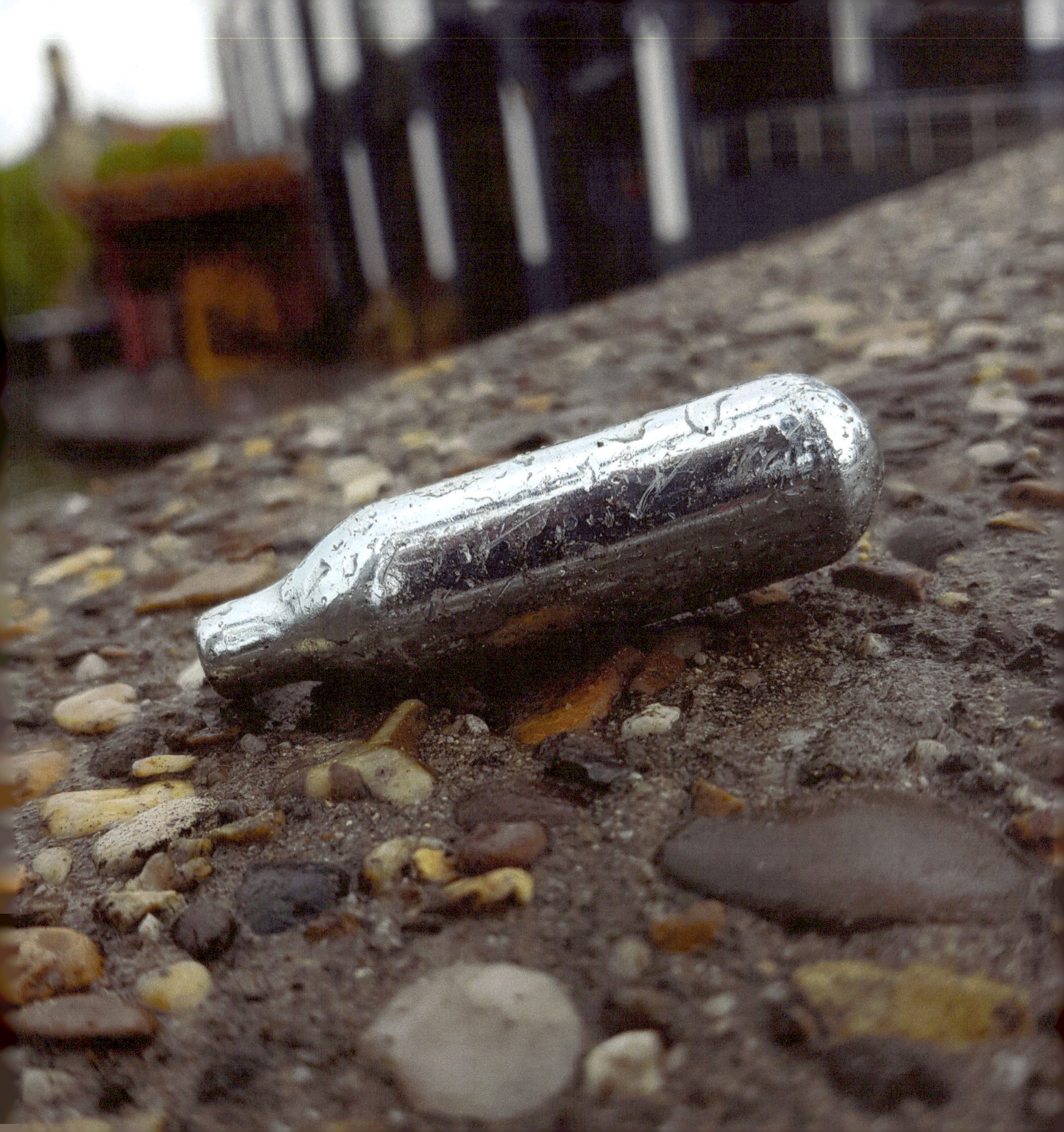

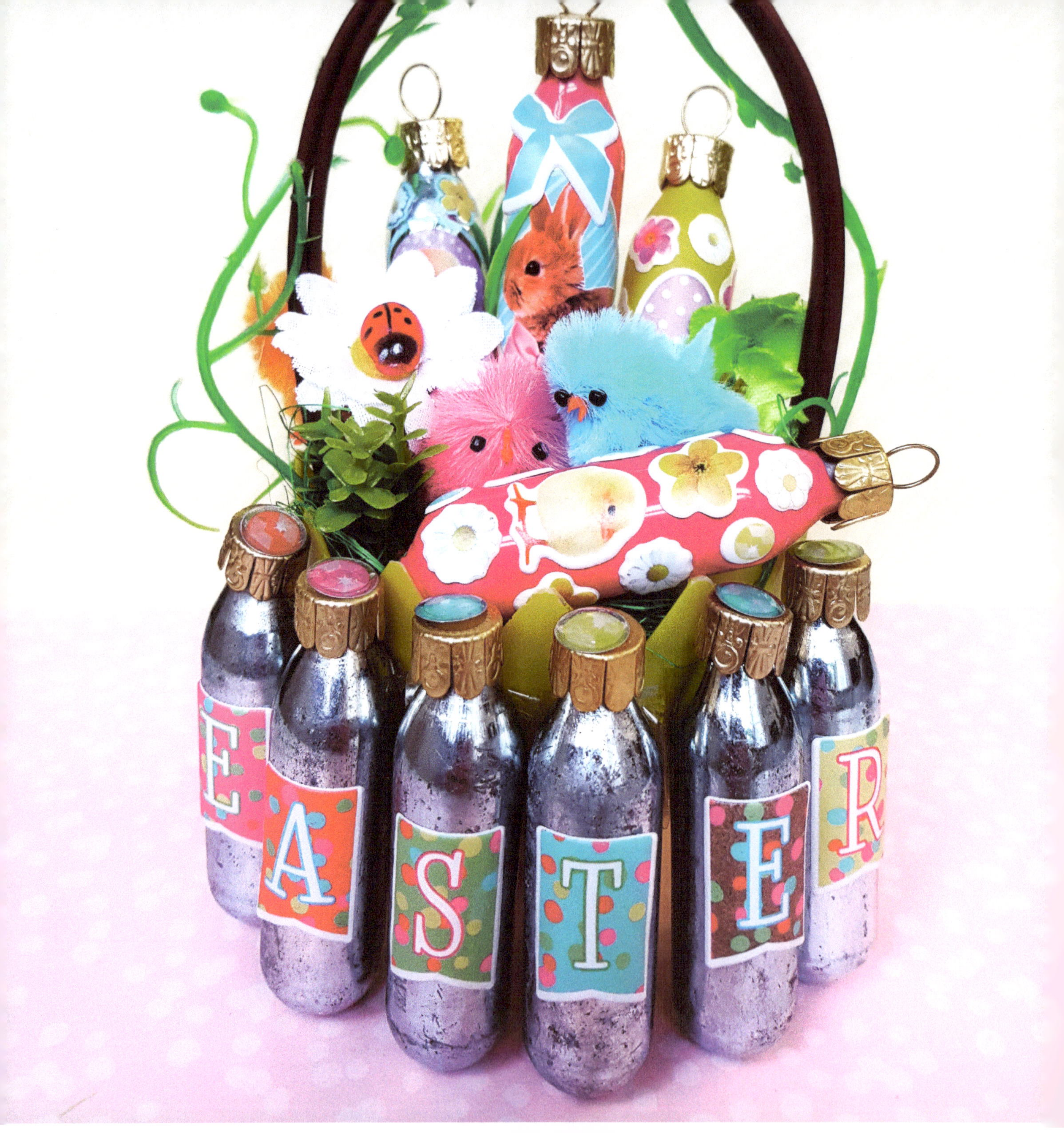
EASTER

STOP THE POLLUTION
& INSPIRE PEOPLE
TO PICK-UP
WHIPPED CREAM
CANISTERS
OF NITROUS OXIDE
JUNKIES
AND MAKE
EASTER DECORATIONS

www.ingramcontent.com/pod-product-compliance
Lightning Source LLC
Chambersburg PA
CBHW042323250526
R18347300001B/R183473PG45473CBX00023B/21
9781718960862